THE WEIGHT OF EMOTIONS

Creating Wellness through Intentional Living

J A R E D   J O N E S

BALBOA.PRESS
A DIVISION OF HAY HOUSE

Balboa Press books may be ordered through booksellers or by contacting:

Balboa Press
A Division of Hay House
1663 Liberty Drive
Bloomington, IN 47403
www.balboapress.com
844-682-1282

Print information available on the last page.

ISBN: 979-8-7652-3969-8 (sc)
ISBN: 979-8-7652-3970-4 (e)

Balboa Press rev. date: 03/24/2023

Contents

Foreword

When I was very young I didn't think about "exercise." The idea of "aerobics" seemed weird. An early memory is watching Olivia Newton John's "Let's Get Physical" music video and wondering "what the heck is that?" At one point my mom purchased a tiny trampoline for "exercise" and we kids were not allowed to play with. Seeing the *Crystal Light Aerobics Championship* on TV produced laughter that has only increased in intensity over the decades. I remember seeing Susan Powter rise to a pop-culture icon with her catchphrase "Stop the Insanity!" while simultaneously thinking to myself, "She kind of comes across as insane!" I wasn't aware at the time that Arnold Schwarzenegger was a decorated bodybuilder and viewed him as only a mediocre actor, famous only because he was jacked. Food guidelines and recommendations have been even more volatile with their ever-changing messages.

Although very young, I recognized the mixed messages and chaos of diet and exercise, and observed as these mixed messages permeated our society and culture. How could there be so many different ways to get to "where we want to be?" And do we really even want or need to "get there," or is "getting there" just something we are *supposed* to want? It's taken me more than 20 years to address and attempt to answer these questions, which serve as the message of this book.

Having worked in the fitness industry for the past two decades, I've seen thousands of books and articles (and have read dozens) about "diet and exercise." The message, reframed with subtle differences, has been the same. Information is repeatedly regurgitated with slightly a different spin. And to put it simply: it hasn't worked, it doesn't work, and it will never work for all of the reasons discussed in this book. We must rethink our approach if our intention is to increase health, wellness, life and happiness.

We can't operate within the same framework and expect to see anything change. Most are familiar with the definition of insanity (usually misattributed to Einstein, and more relatable than Susan Powter's decree to stop it); "doing the same thing over and over again and expecting different results." Most have experienced its applicability in life's relationships, work environments, etc., without being able or willing to make the same kind of connections relative to what we eat and how much we move. It's been shared by countless others: "If nothing changes, nothing changes."

For years, I've been sharing what I've learned that makes people healthier and happier. And I've been encouraged by those I've worked with to share my message, as a new and fresh perspective. To be clear, the research and theories I share are not all uniquely mine, but instead, are integrated in a new way. We constantly learn more about the body and its functions, so we should be regularly and constantly modifying our practices with new information and methods. Additionally, and significantly, every human is a unique biological organism, with unique metabolic factors and considerations. That being true, every food, diet, exercise program, etc., will affect each person differently.

Research is revealing that physical health and overall wellness are so much more than simply "calories in/calories out." We are recognizing the enormous impact that mindset, mental health and emotions have on our eating and exercise habits. I have been reluctant to share my perspective because the information and generally accepted recommendations are so dynamic and changing. But my reluctance has also stemmed from self-limiting thoughts such as: "I'm not an expert," "No one cares about my opinions," "My background is fitness, so I shouldn't talk about nutrition and mindset," "Other voices deserve to be heard before mine…" But I came to realize through questioning these internal dialogues, that I can't expect to share a mindset-centered message, unless I'm operating from the same mindset that I intend to persuade others to embrace. How can I expect others to make changes if I allow fear to hold me hostage?

So, I have decided to take action, to compile my thoughts and opinions to help others to see things from a different perspective. Some of the ideas and concepts in this book are backed by science and research, some are anecdotal, some are theoretical, and will be characterized as such as they are presented, so each reader can pick and choose what resonates with his or her beliefs and goals.

Additionally, and ironically, since starting to write this book, and perhaps partially due to writing this book, I have recently experienced personal and professional setbacks that validate the very message on these pages.

I decided it was time to organize my thoughts in a way that might resonate with others. It is my hope and intention that a fresh perspective on exercise and diet will help others progress to the most authentic version of themselves by incorporating a mindset-foundational, self-actualization model. This will allow every reader to discover that his or her motivations, intention, inspiration — and, ultimately his or her "why" — is greater and more impactful than systems of "hows" that dictate actions and behaviors. And, ultimately (hopefully), these new perspectives and approaches will provide a clearer and more personal path to the flow of health and happiness.

PART 1

"THIS ISN'T WORKING."
SYMPTOMS OF
SICK SYSTEM

STOP "DIETING" AND "EXERCISING"!

"I exercise to lose weight."

"I exercise so I can eat more."

"I exercise so I can drink more."

"I exercise to make up for poor eating choices."

"I exercise because my (doctor/ trainer/ friend/ boss/parent/spouse told me I should."

"I exercise to try to get his/her attention."

"I exercise because I have to for school or work."

As a teacher, trainer and manager of health-related programs I've heard these phrases, and countless others, every day for years.

I don't like exercise. At least, I don't like the word. It's not my intention to diminish the role of "exercise." Obviously, movement is important. *In fact, I believe consistent movement is the single best decision one can make for their overall longevity and health.* But let's talk about the word "exercise." As a fitness professional, I've found it more effective to point out that the statements above are all outcome-based — they usually connote an outcome as motivation rather than a process for becoming healthier and happier.

At this point you may be thinking, "Well, of course, the ultimate goal is to be happier." But incremental goals based on temporary and/or superficial factors and metrics won't "get you there." The foundational principle of this book is to examine the "why" more than the "how." And our "whys" can only be conditioned on *personal choices, actions, behaviors and thoughts; not others' expectations*, if we want to get the most out of what we are doing, and if we want to find *Flow*, what I define as living with inspired intention.

A big problem, however, is that changing our outcome-based mindset is much easier said than done. We have been conditioned our whole lives to believe certain things about diet, exercise, and our bodies. We've been taught that exercise and diet are important only in relation to outcomes that, in most cases, are not supported by science or experience. This societal, familial, and cultural conditioning is due to *beliefs and behavior* rather than *biology*.

We are judged, and sometimes defined, by how we look and perform in our competitive/comparison society. As children we compete with friends and siblings. In grade school we continue the pattern, adding peer judgment and expectations, which sometimes enables vicious bullying. At recess, we "pick teams" based on the "most valuable player available" and "popularity" model(s). We distinguish winners and losers and assign meaning to those designations. And because of those designations we are taught to feel good or bad based on the outcome, regardless of personal preferences. Lacking maturity, we fail to ask ourselves this question: *Should I feel bad because I was on a "losing team" even though I had no choice of team, in a class I don't enjoy, playing a game I don't care about?*

Even environments intended to instill a love of the body and movement, like Physical Education, are inherently flawed. As a former PE teacher, I always struggled with some colleagues who used exercise as punishment (a student late to class, or not properly dressed being told "go run a lap," or "do 20 burpees"). The teacher unknowingly and inadvertently becomes a "bully." And so, our conditioning to associate exercise with outcomes begins early. And it's doubly damaging because the association is usually negative–reinforcing a belief that movement is not "regular" or "normal." As a result, "exercise" exposes more limitations than practices, habits, and behaviors that contribute to living a fuller life.

Further along life's path, we start to learn and adopt the flawed paradigm that dictates and validates this misguided and usually non-purposeful approach. This flawed paradigm will be discussed in later chapters, but as a preview, we exercise for all the wrong reasons, because that's what we're taught and "know."

The starting place to a better approach is two-fold: 1) Identify our real motivation, inspiration and "Why" while, 2) replacing the outcome-focused approaches to the way we eat and why/how we move.

Again, it's much easier said than done, because, when it comes to diet and exercise, motivation is usually born of either fear, a sense of obligation/duty, or to satisfy others' expectations.

Acting out of fear doesn't mean we are scared; but instead, are acting to subvert something negative. Phrases associated with fear regarding diet and exercises are "I have to" and or "I can't."

"I am doing '75-Hard' and must get my second workout in today!"

"I'm on the Keto diet so I can't eat that banana!"

When acting out of obligation, we hear phrases that include words like "should" and "shouldn't."

"I shouldn't eat that last bite."

"I should go on a walk to make sure I get my steps in."

I believe "obligation" statements are watered-down fear-based statements. The language used makes the action seem more justified but still demonstrates little interest in and/or commitment to the action or behavior. But both fear and obligation are conditional and external motivators. As such, they can't be effective in developing a sustainable long-term plan! Fear holds us hostage to others' standards, protocols, expectations, etc. Additionally, fear-based motivation allows for excuses when results inevitably plateau or when the program didn't deliver on the promised outcomes.

Conversely, when we operate out of "love" we use phrases like "I want to", and "I'd rather not". Operating from "love" means we are living in accordance with who we feel we authentically are and moving in the direction of self-actualization or purpose. When operating from a place of love, we eat the way we eat, and move the way we move regardless of the outcome.

Unless and until we choose to be motivated through love, any program, system, and associated results will be short-term, limited and unsustainable. Not to mention devoid of joy.

Before examining, critiquing, selecting or evaluating any system of exercise or diet, start by asking two simple questions: "What do I want to accomplish by changing my behavior, and WHY do I want to accomplish that goal?" We must recognize that our WHY is greater than our HOW. The well-known neurologist, psychiatrist, philosopher, author, and Holocaust survivor Viktor Frankl is credited saying "He who has a 'why' can bear any 'how'."

Until we begin our mindset-approach by asking ourselves these key questions, we continue in the vicious cycles of yo-yo dieting and exercise – chasing results validated through others' expectations. Instead, we must shift our goals to living with intention and direction, because living according to our own choices is what invites joy into our lives.

Try this exercise: Make a list of the last few diets and exercise programs you have tried. After listing them, write the pros and cons of each (based on your observations, knowledge and experience). What did they provide? What did they "cost" (energy, passion, time, money etc.)? In doing so, it is rare that we identify factors that are not conditioned on an outcome.

It would be difficult to convince me that "love" was someone's motivation for following the "Cabbage Soup Diet." I doubt anyone has ever uttered "I love cabbage soup so much that it's all I want to eat for the rest of my life…" Many diets even warn participants against the long-term effects of the eating patterns they advocate!

We see the same patterns in fitness. Most exercise programs and systems have conditions. 'P90X' is 90 days. '75 hard' is 75 days. Weight-loss competitions are time-banded and tied to an outcome, etc.

"Exercise" however, is a cultural phenomenon. Our ancestors didn't wake up early to go to the gym or run. The idea of needlessly expending energy would have been ridiculous! Our bodies have evolved with instincts to conserve energy and simplify all facets of sustaining life. As hunter-gatherers and farmers, we balanced our energy consumption to match our energy output.

To explore the cultural argument further, imagine introducing body-fat, muscle-mass, and/or bone-density testing to an indigenous people, separate from modern/western influence. Being told "based on the data you could benefit from decreasing body fat 3% and adding 5 pounds of muscle" it would not be received with any level of understanding and/or scope. If we asked the Tarahumara people (written about in the book "Born to Run") to run on treadmills to measure their gait and physiological markers like VO2 Max, recovery heart rate, blood lactate, etc., and attempted to present them with the information, the context would be lost on them! Both examples indicate that those of us who focus on the culturally accepted outcome-focus of diet and exercise are historically in the global minority, and… we are doing it the wrong way: devolving instead of evolving. Enduring through fear instead of living and flowing in joy.

Today, energy is abundant, and we don't have to work for it. We sleep more and do so in comfortable beds. We wake up and prepare a rich meal with food we didn't directly produce. We shower with hot water that requires no effort other than turning a handle. Even our toothbrushes do the work for us. We drive to our place of employment, ride an escalator or elevator to our office where we sit for eight hours a day, moving only to go to the bathroom or consume more energy (that usually exponentially exceeds what is required, and is less nutrient dense). Then we follow these steps in reverse until bedtime when the cycle starts over. The cultural conditioning and technological advances we "enjoy" today have completely altered our evolutionary progress and instincts.

The ease and availability of food (some of which barely qualifies to be called such) coupled with living in systems that require little to no movement have created the perfect storm for disease and illness. As a result, we must add intentional movement to offset the negative impacts of regular life; a scenario described perfectly in the Daniel Lieberman's book title: "Exercised: Why Something We Never Evolved to Do is Healthy and Rewarding."

Recent research has strengthened the previously theoretical hypothesis that our "whys" and "beliefs" about our health-related behaviors are more closely associated with efficacy than "what" those practices are! Stated more simply, if we think the way we are eating is the healthiest option, our bodies will respond to our thoughts, in addition to responding to the nutrients in the food.

While listening to a podcast recently I was introduced to Dr. Alia Crum and the research she and her team are engaged in. She spent years researching the placebo and nocebo effects of drugs on our physiology. She became interested as to whether our thoughts and beliefs on what we were eating would also change our physiological processes. It's a question that many in the field of physiology and dietetics would have scoffed at until Crum's team conducted what she called "the milkshake study."

Dr. Crum mixed one batch of vanilla milkshakes, and then divided that singular batch into two others, and labeled the two smaller batches differently. One sub-batch was put into bottles labeled as "Sensishake" — a healthy and balanced shake with 140 calories and no added fat or sugar. The remainder was put into bottles that were advertised as a dessert shake, they called "Indulgence" with a label boasting 620 calories and loaded with fat and sugar. The truth, known only to the researchers, was that the identical shakes had the same 300 total calories. The researchers used Ghrelin (the hunger hormone) as their metric to determine if perception influenced physiology. Participants had their Ghrelin levels measured both before and after drinking their shakes. The intention here is not to explain how Ghrelin assists in regulation of hunger but instead share the results. Crum discovered those who believed they were drinking the higher calorie "Indulgence" displayed a physiological response of being "fuller" and "satisfied." Crum summarized, "The ghrelin levels dropped about three times more when people were consuming the indulgent shake (or thought they were consuming the indulgent shake), compared to the people who drank the sensible shake (or thought that's what they were drinking)."

Dr. Crum took her now-validated research hypothesis to see if it could be replicated in perception of the benefits of "exercise." Since it would obviously be much more difficult to convince someone that they were or were not exercising, she worked with physically active housekeepers. Half received education on general fitness recommendations and were shown that their jobs met and exceeded those recommendations. The results were similar. Housekeepers who were told about the health benefits of their jobs lost weight, felt better, and were classified as being happier in their work!

We all benefit from and have a need to move more, but "why" we want to be a healthier version of ourselves is much more important than "how" we get there. And the more we focus on enjoying the process (participating in things we enjoy and would participate in regardless of outcome), the happier we will be, AND the faster we will get where (at present think) we want to be.

We will discuss motivation as well as different approaches to eating and moving to help us get there, but first, we need to dig a little deeper how we got to this place of misunderstanding, miscommunication and misguided misery.

2

A FLAWED PARADIGM

Given a choice, most humans choose routine and resist change. New concepts, ideas and approaches challenge us. But our inability to adapt *may* prevent our individual and collective health and progress. What if most of what we think we know about diet and exercise is both outdated and theoretical? If so, would we change our approach, or just repackage our "knowledge" in new, flashier ways that ultimately lead to the same result(s)?

"Weight" has become the go-to metric that most use to determine where they are on their health and wellness journey. I believe weight is the least important measure as you will come to understand. We have been taught that weight is the key to health, and that "losing weight" and "increasing health" are somewhat synonymous. In fact, the correlation is not always substantiated by research. Although very limited, the association between weight and health is the foundation of the flawed paradigm in which many live. We are told that if we are not the ideal weight we are "less-than"— that to be "healthy" we must lose weight by dieting, exercise, or a combination of both.

The "ideal diet" has changed over decades, along with different approaches to fitness. Although the message has changed, the outcomes and goals have remained the same, and most people eat and exercise based solely on the belief that these actions will help maintain and/or lose weight; and, in return, that will somehow increase happiness.

Because the foundation is based on misunderstood correlations and theories, it spawns a vicious cycle of short-lived patterns and behaviors to change a symptom rather than the root cause. This misunderstanding and misinterpretation of fundamental concepts also gave birth to the capitalization of health. Presently, the nutrition, supplement, fitness, and equipment industries are founded on selling products and services despite having little to do with actual physical health.

As a result, we live with a system, consisting of unregulated industries, and unqualified people, controlling and communicating the "weight=health" message. After convincing the general population that weight is the problem, those same industries disingenuously create the solution(s) to their self-defined problem. So many embark on a life-long cycle of trial and error; not out of lack of trying, or desire, but rather because the message is inconsistent, and based on false or outdated hypotheses.

The industry has created a business model rather than a health model. We live in a system of sales and revenue instead of health and wellness.

To support this model the industry uses expectations as the main driving and motivational force — expectations that are typically not related to being healthier, but rather looking a certain way or making us become or obtain something we currently aren't, or lack. With expectations come guilt, shame, frustration and the other negative emotions that ensure we keep coming back for the latest and greatest, flashiest and newest.

In "How to Hug a Porcupine," author John Lund writes: "Remember all frustration is based on unmet expectations. If we did not expect anything, we would not be frustrated."

Statistically only 26% of women and 28% of men are happy with the way they look; meaning nearly three-fourths of the population is frustrated and would like to improve the way they look.

If we honestly ask ourselves: "Where do my outcome-based expectations, regarding health, fitness, body, etc. come from? It doesn't take long to realize that they do not come from within. We are not born inherently ashamed of the way we look. We find that our expectations come from the claims, words, and feedback of others. Everyone and everything *else*, whether we consciously realize it, is influencing our thoughts, behaviors and actions.

That vast majority of the population who are dissatisfied with where they are provides a huge market for products and services that, in many cases, are not even based on health, and use fear, guilt and shame to consistently introduce and modify expectations by peddling their products and/or services.

An article in 'Entrepreneur' titled "The two Psychological Factors Motivating Customers to Buy" articulates this idea. The equation to motivate to 'sell' is:

Current Dissatisfaction x Future Promise > Cost + Fear.

Since a majority of us are dissatisfied with how we look and feel, the promise of losing *weight* as the cure for that dissatisfaction leads to believing that almost any cost is worth it, especially when compounded by the fear of not acting soon enough.

Television shows with weight and weight-loss in their titles capitalize on the weight=health message and are sometimes a thin disguise for the real message that weight=guilt/shame. They award prizes and money for those who "succeed" and send others home who didn't meet expectations. No one wants to watch a "reality" show that is based on realistic weekly weight-loss goals of one to two pounds (be honest; you wouldn't watch that show) and sponsors wouldn't support or produce that message. So, to make it more entertaining, they condense three to four weeks of material into weekly episodes, as well as using all the "dirty tricks of the trade" to inflate and deflate numbers at weigh-ins and weigh-outs. Not to make it healthier. Not to make it more realistic, but instead to simply make it more entertaining. Meanwhile, at home, viewers start to develop an expectation that "if only I could be on that show," "if only I could work out with that trainer," or "if only I could eat that exact diet," etc., I could have the same (unrealistic) results.

Infomercials and advertisements for diet and exercise products and programs use the same model: create an expectation, provide a unique solution to the expectation (by any means necessary without providing substantiation of the problem or the solution) and use fear to create urgency in the moment to purchase that program or service.

It's not new, we've seen it a thousand times, but it doesn't prevent us from falling for it again and again because the expectations are so high, and tied to the emotions that govern our self-worth. So, we continue buying the latest, trendiest, and greatest; while bottles and tubs of half-used powders and pills fill our cupboards and pantries, and DVD workouts gather dust on the shelf, and the treadmill in the corner becomes a laundry rack.

It's a foolproof business model because it's driven by emotion. The expectation, and what we believe that expectation would 'make' us, is so powerful that we keep coming back for more, even when the promised results are not realized.

Perhaps the root of it all stems from the dumbed-down and many-times debunked theory of metabolic energy balance - the simple mathematical application of calories-in vs. calories-out.

The mythical, mathematical approach to weight loss

In my first personal training job, the head trainer sat down with me and said, "This is how you sell personal training," not "This is how you become the best trainer you can be to help your clients reach their goals." At the time, I didn't see the glaring inconsistency in front of me; that my job was more about selling my services, than about helping others (and, by extension, myself).

He outlined the plan: "There are 3,500 calories in a pound of fat. If one wants to lose weight, they need to achieve a daily caloric deficit. To lose one pound of fat per week, that person needs to create a caloric deficit of 500 calories per day."

(500 calories/day x seven days = 3500 calories, or one pound of fat) He went on to explain that the caloric deficit could come from diet (eating less) OR exercise (moving more) OR a combination of both.

It was so simple! And I was so excited to start changing lives with this new revelatory information! The only problem: it's all completely theoretical nonsense. It shouldn't matter that it's easy to communicate if it doesn't work! There are many factors that make it not that simple.

The first should be obvious. Every human is biologically unique. No two people have identical metabolic factors. Age, gender, height, ethnicity, amount of muscle, amount of fat, muscle and fat distribution, health/medical conditions, hormonal balance, environment, emotions, etc., are all factors that implicate how, and where our bodies store fat, as well as convert fat into energy.

Another thing to consider is our natural inclination to believe 'if a little is good, more must be better.' This is called "compounding the factors." One may look at the math and say "I'm not happy with a pound a week, so if i can create a 1,000 daily caloric deficit it will result in 2 pounds! 1,500 calories a day = 3 pounds a week! Five pounds by creating a 2,500-calorie deficit each day! This is a dangerous slippery slope that may lead to disordered eating patterns and exercise addiction; not to mention the frustration when one realizes that the energy and effort haven't translated to the expected result!

Yet another basic human instinct affects calorie counting. We overestimate what we perceive to be our positive characteristics, and underestimate those less-positive factors. We almost always overestimate our caloric output (exercise/activity), and undercount what we take in.

And the most important for exposing flaws in simple mathematical weight loss is the idea that all calories are equal. "Nutrient density" and the quality of our nutrition speaks volumes more than the sheer number of calories alone.

If all of those factors weren't enough, perhaps the most poignant factor is the calories-in/calories-out approach falsely purports a 1:1 ratio of calories expended in exercise to a calorie stored as potential energy. The simple truth that exposes this fallacy is that the metabolic processes which our bodies use to take in and store energy are very different from the metabolic processes our bodies use to convert that energy into movement.

Think about it! If weight loss could be determined by a simple equation, there would be no "weight-loss competitions" because the results could be determined by math. In environments like fitness resorts, guests eat the same food and exercise the same amounts (within a margin of error). If simple mathematics applied, we would expect to see consistent results (within those same margins of error). But that is not, and cannot be the case, because even with a controlled caloric deficit, it is impossible to pre-determine individual results because of varied individual biological factors.

This isn't a popular message for the industries who've created it. It's much harder to sell reality than hope. Even with this knowledge, real change must happen on an individual basis, as the inaccurate and false beliefs we hold are deep-rooted in who we are as a society.

In fact, the misguided messages are so ingrained into our beliefs and behaviors, it has lasting and impactful effects even on the lives of those like me who don't buy into the generally accepted message! My unwillingness to perpetuate the fallacy by ignorantly and blindly repeating what I know to be false, led to my departure from what I thought and hoped was my dream job. It was devastating for me to leave a job that I was good at and that I loved due to challenging the status quo.

Once we realize that most of "what" we are doing in regard to diet and exercise is flawed, it allows space for new information and new approaches to the way we eat and move. Ones that are more individual and authentic to our lives and greater good. Once we realize our motivation has been coming from outside for-profit businesses using fear and obligation, it allows for space to create new systems for ourselves from a place of love, that are more aligned with who we are and what we really want.

3

UNINTENDED DAMAGES OF THE FLAWED PARADIGM

In addition to all the fallacies that are embedded within the flawed paradigm just discussed, we should also examine our behaviors in response to the mixed-misinformation messaging; especially as it relates to the different approaches to wellness forthcoming. Because the paradigm isn't based on science or health, it ultimately sets us up, individually and collectively, to fail. With that perceived failure, comes feelings of shame and guilt. These negative emotions can be a catalyst to all kinds of behaviors that can take us further away from where we want to be. Practices that are considered acceptable, healthful, and beneficial, can have the opposite effect when they originate from a place of lack, guilt or shame.

Addiction

A few years ago, I listened to a TED talk by Johann Hari titled "Everything you think you know about addiction is wrong." Although a bold claim, the title rang true to me. The premise of Hari's presentation was ultimately "the opposite of addiction is not sobriety, but connection." Therefore, disconnection from self and others, however it manifests in each of us, is a main contributor to addiction. We seek to fill those perceived voids within us with behaviors that allow us to feel in control of our outcomes and life.

The behaviors we use as coping mechanisms compound the disconnect to ourselves and others by altering vital parts of our personality that make us who we are. Addiction impacts our self-awareness — our capacity to know ourselves through identifying and understanding our emotions, thoughts, feelings, motives, strengths and weaknesses as they relate to feeling "safe." Addiction impacts our ability to self-regulate our wellness baseline and behaviors, including feeling in-control of emotional responses to stimuli, sleep patterns, appetite, and other bodily functions. These individual and incremental losses of autonomy compound, causing even deeper disconnection to self and others, as well as dependency on the substance, practice or behavior.

Another pioneer at the forefront of addiction research is Gabor Mate. He says: "If we want to understand addiction, we cannot look at what is wrong with the addiction, we must look at what is right about it; in other words what is the person getting from the addiction? What void is the addiction providing that otherwise they don't have?" Examining that question, we find that addictions provide many people a (temporary) feeling of control, peace, and relief from pain — sometimes physical but, in many cases, emotional. So, the question shouldn't be "Why is addiction becoming more prevalent?" but instead, "Why is pain increasing?" The answer then is not found in a person's genetics, but instead in his or her life experience. The more pain, suffering, and trauma one has experienced, the higher their susceptibility to addiction and addictive behaviors.

Many times, there is a clear relationship between physical and/or sexual abuse and substance addiction. I believe the same kind of association can be made between addiction and years of yo-yo dieting and exercise. Failing to meet promised outcomes may immerse one in guilt and shame and, ultimately, without recognizing the long-term damage, to addictive behaviors to regain control and peace of mind. Just as we pass abuse and trauma from one generation to the next, by allowing false narratives to persist we also pass along unrealistic health standards. This ironically compounds the unhealthiness of individuals and society. For example, we know that many health metrics and factors we consider are more behavioral than biological but use biology as a crutch because it validates our beliefs that our actions are beyond our control, when the exact opposite is the truth.

Body Dysmorphia

When tracing the origins of the culturally accepted health standards, we recognize quickly and easily how ridiculous they are. Without demeaning all pageants, they provide an example of our misguided superficial approach to our bodies. When I was younger, many young girls dreamed about "Miss America." Pageants like this continue to be gender specific, which is a subject for exploration in and of itself. That aside, I believe the most troublesome aspect of these competitions is the swimsuit portion. As pageant standards have changed, this portion has been re-branded "Fitness in Swimsuit" and other titles. It's obviously ridiculous to believe that any accurate assessment or assumption can be made about a person's health simply by how they look in a swimsuit while walking across a stage and waiving. This is another iteration of the fallacy of using weight as a metric of health. A result is hundreds of thousands of girls and young women with dreams of being Miss (insert community or school here) sacrificing their health to impress a judge that they are "healthy" instead of being healthy.

We are not born with a compulsion to look a certain way, or to feel bad if we don't look that way. It is a conditioned response created by our environment. And we sacrifice our health, our happiness, and lives to achieve outcomes that aren't healthy and will not lead us to where we really want to be. We judge ourselves harshly and adopt practices that become habits and then compulsions, to achieve the result that we think will bring us happiness and remove the guilt and shame we've become accustomed to and accepted. It's another vicious cycle that prevents us from finding the flow of authentic self-actualization and happiness.

Hormonal Havoc

The "dumbing-down" of the messaging around weight-loss and the flawed paradigm have led to a gross simplification of metabolism. We do ourselves a disservice by increasing our frustration when approaching weight-loss from the perspective of outcomes instead of processes (adopting the disproved calories-in/calories-out equation). Metabolism is a complex combination of biological processes dependent on a complex network of interdependent muscles and organs that spark other complex biological responses and processes! It's all complex. And it's all individual.

Most "diets' or patterned eating programs designed to decrease weight use the manipulation of regulatory hormonal metabolic processes to achieve outcomes. The more we change our diets to achieve an outcome, the more we force our bodies to work in ways it has not evolved to work. For example, let's look at the "high-protein diets." However branded, (Atkins, The Zone, Paleo, Keto, etc.) all are based on the premise that removing carbohydrates from the diet forces the body to use fat for energy. What often isn't discussed is that eliminating carbohydrates from the diet also removes the body's natural hormonal response to metabolizing carbohydrates. This effect may be positive for some and negative for others, depending on many factors. Without discussing specific diets, all should be aware that focusing on validating the efficacy of a particular weight-loss regimen may lead us to initially ignore individual factors. By removing a complete macronutrient source (protein, carbohydrate, fat) from our diet, we also eliminate, or at least limit, the body's natural hormonal metabolic responses to that macronutrient.

The more drastic the eating-pattern change in fad dieting, the harder it is for a body to determine its metabolic homeostasis. Without regulatory hormonal processes, we can't adapt fast enough and as a result, get discouraged. The result is continually chasing temporary diets with temporary results, rather than taking actions to create habits and systems of lifelong health and body-composition management.

I've heard folks in my line of work say things like "I've lost thousands of pounds over my lifetime." The pattern of yo-yo dieting and exercise-program hopping has become the norm, the standard, the status quo. Many may ask "what is the harm in cycling patterns of eating and exercise?" Because of the results and outcome-focused nature of diet and exercise, we may not always pay attention to other things that may be going on with our bodies.

Procrastinating Progress

The health=weight paradigm discussed earlier also provides the perfect environment for procrastination in our lives. Human beings naturally seek ease and work to avoid pain, suffering and conflict. The constant flow of mixed-messaging about health, fitness and weight loss supports outcome-focused metrics. Clearly defined outcomes and expectations require clearly defined starting points and protocols. But if we don't enjoy the activity, food, exercise, etc., our nature is to find excuses to delay starting. We usually opt to start something new "tomorrow morning," or "next Monday," or the "first of next month," or "with the new year."

How many times has our natural inclination to avoid a challenge or hardship been stronger than our motivation to begin?

Process-focused habits and goals don't require outcomes, so there's no need to assign a start date. Process-focused goals allow for living in the present, and for recognizing the literal impact of every daily decision, action, and thought. This will be discussed in Chapter 7 "Living with Intention."

Loss Of, And Barriers To Discovering, Autonomy

Autonomy and self-governance are values that can allow each person to answer, "Who am I?" Unfortunately, this unhealthy weight=health paradigm tells each of us "who we are" without even considering all the traits and characteristics that make us unique and who we actually are. The environment and circumstances of the status quo dictate who we are, relieving us of doing the work ourselves, and barring us from living to discover the contrast toward self-actualization and autonomy. So this false paradigm represents both a loss of autonomy and prevents self-discovery. This will also be discussed in greater length and detail in later chapters.

Chasing Perfectionism

When cultural and societal standards dictate the expectations and practices promised for what society says is "healthy," the result is a population chasing an "ideal," or "perfection." But perfection is not a literal objective, but rather a figurative representation! Since we are all unique biological organisms with unique strengths, weaknesses, interests, goals etc., each person's "ideal" or "perfect" should also be just as unique, a stark contrast to the cookie-cutter reality we live in.

4

FINDING FLOW AND
IDENTIFYING OUR 'WHYS'

The concept of "Flow" is one Mihaly Csikszentmihalyi introduced in his groundbreaking work: "Flow: The Psychology of Optimal Experience" as the process of cultivating authentic joy in our lives. He explains that "Happiness is not rigid but does require consistent intention and effort. Happiness is therefore an internal state of being, not an external one." Additionally, his research showed that each of us are most creative, productive, and happy when we are in a state of flow!

So, what is Flow? And more important, how do we each find our state of flow? The following pages are filled with "how," but let's dig deeper into what a "flow state" is.

Csikszentmihalyi defined Flow as: "a state in which people are so involved in an activity that nothing else seems to matter; the experience is so enjoyable that people will continue to do it even at great cost, for the sheer sake of doing it" (1990).

How many of us can (truthfully) say that we eat the way we eat and move the way we move simply because we enjoy it? I would argue that the opposite is more common – that most of us exercise and eat in ways we don't enjoy at all, resulting in habits based on promised, and usually elusive, results.

To reach and maintain flow-states, we must be aware of our purpose(s), or "why(s)," to serve as direction and focus for our intention and effort.

So, let's consider WHYs. Why do we want to become a better version of ourselves? Why do we want to lose weight? Why do we want to be stronger? Why do we want to be more flexible, more mobile, run faster or longer? Why are we dieting? Why are we even exercising?

Without consciously identifying the core reasons behind what we are doing, we will robotically continue the cycle of yo-yo dieting and exercise-program hopping indefinitely chasing something elusive without acknowledging or understanding the real motivation behind our actions and behaviors. And if we don't understand the motivations behind the facade, we will repeat the same patterns, and hit the same speed bumps and roadblocks that inevitably lead to the same outcomes and frustrations.

The overwhelmingly most common – and most misguided – response to the question "Why do you exercise and/or diet?" is "to lose weight." But "losing weight" is not a "why." Nor can it be!

Why can't weight be a metric to flow-state? Because a number on a scale simply provides no information about "health." And even if it did, it would be only one marker of hundreds. Weight says nothing about a *person*. It says nothing about who he or she is; nothing about values, background, struggles, goals, etc. Measuring weight doesn't even provide information about health! It says nothing about amounts of fat or muscle; nothing about cardiorespiratory endurance; nothing about flexibility and mobility; nothing about immune system strength, or digestive regularity, or cognitive function. The list goes on and on what we 'think' weight represents, but the fact is, it's a single metric measuring the force of a body in relation to gravity. Yet many use it on a daily (or even more frequently) as if it were a continual indication of personal worth or value. Even if weight provided "health-related" information, it, of course, would still not say anything of one's worth and value, and therefore can only hinder one's pursuit for flow state.

Each person must discover that it's not in the number, but rather what that number represents to each of us. It's easier said than done because we have been taught and conditioned our whole lives that there is value in that number, where there is, quite simply and unequivocally, not.

Let's compare the outcome of "weight-loss" to the outcome of receiving money. Most of us welcome money in our lives, and it's a driving factor for many. We are not overly critical of the way money comes into our lives and most would love more money. But it's not the actual bills, coins or credit we want, but rather what money represents: value! More money (a medium of exchange) means more ability to acquire abundance, or the experiences that contribute to abundant lives. Just as money represents something different – different possessions, experiences, security – to every person, the meaning of "weight loss" is different for every person.

I've been immersed in the industry for years. I've been blessed to work with thousands of people on their health journeys, and it STILL makes me cringe when people say: "I want to lose weight." It makes me cringe because they're using a metric that does not implicitly lead to the outcomes they want, but is instead a conditioned response that, in most cases, creates more problems and roadblocks than progress and solutions. But in EVERY case, IT'S NOT ABOUT THE WEIGHT!

It's not about the weight because weight can't be the real motivation; instead, it is the societal condition we think will put us in a position where we want to be. I've found that the number on a scale comes to represent to each person something greater than the number itself! That's where the discussion must start if we wish to break the cycle that has plagued our experience and stifled our progress to a better version of self.

Earlier in my career, I was fortunate to be introduced to a therapy model called Dialectical Behavior Therapy (DBT). DBT is a branch of Cognitive Behavior Therapy that teaches us to live in the present and regulate emotions to improve our relationship with self and others. It's evolved as an evidence- based approach to treat numerous conditions and has applications in both group and individual therapy models. I don't intend to go deeper into DBT other than to acknowledge that it introduced me to an emotion-regulation practice that, to me, serves as the perfect model to understand our motivations. It also helps us dig a little deeper into what drives our thoughts, behaviors and actions, especially in cultivating our "why" in relation to the number on the scale. That practice is known as a Branch Chain Analysis.

A Branch Chain Analysis (BCA) is the practice of asking ourselves (additional) clarifying questions about our thoughts, beliefs and behaviors until we uncover the real reason, catalyst, or stimulus that motivates a desire to change.

> *Below is a sample dialogue that represents the method:*
>
> **I want to lose weight...**
>
> *Why?*
>
> **My doctor told me I need to.**
>
> *Why?*
>
> **Because if I don't, I will suffer health problems that could lead to death.**
>
> *Why is it important to live longer and be healthy?*
>
> **I want to be around for my kids and grandkids.**
>
> *Why?*
>
> **Because I value family and there are things, I would like to do with them.**
>
> *Like what?*
>
> **I love skiing.**
>
> *Where do you like to ski?*

Alta Ski Resort.

So, it's not about weight?

No! I want to be able to ski with my great grandkids at Alta Ski Resort when I'm in my 80's!

Another method to help one find her or his "why" or motivation is to do an emotional identification activity. Emotions are our body's way of communicating messages to us and will be discussed further in later chapters as well as practices outlined in part 2 of this book.

Regardless of how we get there, it is imperative that we do this hard work. Understanding our motivations is not only foundational, but also necessary if our goal is creating a life of health and happiness, and is the basis of the following chapter.

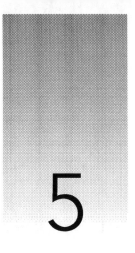

5

WHY OUR "WHYS" MATTER

We will never get to where we think we want to be unless we first start from a place of complete and unconditional love for ourselves in the present.

If we can't look ourselves in the mirror and authentically exclaim "I love me" and mean and feel it, more exercise and a perfect diet won't matter. We will never reach a place of peace or joy with our health or body because we are constantly chasing moving targets based on others' opinions, standards, expectations and ideals. Ironically, when we achieve that level of unconditional self-love – that flow-state – we are no longer focused on "Where we want to be." We are unconditionally content where we are!

The flawed paradigm discussed earlier has conditioned us to believe our physical bodies are a reflection of who we are. While we each have the power to create the lives we desire, our reality is filled with judgment and expectations from almost everyone and everything in our lives. Even though we may easily admit to flaws in our past thinking patterns, observing them in our present selves is usually difficult. Seeds planted early in life followed by years and decades of reinforcing patterns and thoughts, allow those fragile seeds to take root and strengthen. But they do not have to define who we are. We are not our bodies, and our bodies do not define who we are. We are not our injuries and our injuries do not define who we are. We are not our limitations or conditions, and our limitations and conditions do not define us.

Letting go of others' expectations for, and opinions about, us and our lives can be liberating, and is necessary if we intend to reach a flow-state. Doing so can allow each of us to discover, create and define ourselves! We find love and peace for ourselves regardless of what everyone else expects – regardless of others' opinions, regardless of any physical metric. The alternative to finding love for self, independent of all external validation or criticism, is an unhappy cycle of living based on others' ideals and values.

This is not easy, and in many cases feels the opposite of "natural;" however this "unnatural" feeling is also a result of societal and cultural conditioning that has dictated our thoughts and emotions about our bodies and health.

Think about it; when a baby is born, we often use the word "perfect" and, in every case, those children are just that, perfect!

Not all babies are born in perfect health, with the same weight, height, etc. Each child is unique and, as a result, a perfect version of her/himself. When do we replace that natural non-judgment with shallow assumptions and uneducated judgments? More importantly *WHY* do we choose to look for perceived imperfections in others, to seemingly bolster how we feel about ourselves?

We are not born with an innately shameful attitude about our appearances; but that is exactly where the cultural and societal conditioning has led most of us. As a result, our ability to tap into how we *feel* is limited, especially our ability to feel positively about ourselves. This is a great paradoxical dilemma of our wellness journeys; the ability to "feel" what our bodies are communicating, and our ability to interpret those feelings, is really where the journey must start, regardless of what the catalyst is.

How we think and feel about our health and our physical bodies may have greater implications to our health and bodies than our dietary and exercise habits and behaviors. So, if we don't start from a place of self-love (regardless of our perceived imperfections) then we will never get to "where we want to be," because "where we want to be" isn't really what *we* want, but rather it's what *we think we should* want, AND because of that, the external and moving target is impossible to catch or obtain.

6

MOTIVATION VS. INSPIRATION

Having briefly discussed the difference(s) between internal and external motivation, as well as the differences between being motivated by fear, obligation and love, let's examine why "motivation" alone still may not be enough; and spoiler alert, it's not discipline either.

If the goal is to eliminate the outcome-focused approach in wellness, and to then develop habits allowing a life of living in the moment, motivation can't ever be enough, since motivation to act is based on carrying an idea or thought to its logical conclusion; and conclusion is synonymous with outcome.

That is, if we're internally motivated, or driven – even by self-love and growth – we still harbor expectations of outcomes.

Instead of motivation, real clarity comes through purpose-driven *inspiration*. Of course, motivation is a starting point to help find our inspiration, but ultimately real change and growth, consistent and over time, can only come from personal inspiration.

In a former training job, I loved teaching a class that came at the end of an already physically and emotionally challenging week. Participants often arrived at class with comments like "I don't know how much I'm going to be able to do here" and "I'm completely spent, I'm going to be happy just to finish." But every week, something amazing happened. During the class each participant connected with something deep inside themselves to challenge themselves and overcome (perceived) physical and emotional barriers. In some cases, they set personal bests. In every case, every person left having done more than they thought possible only 45 minutes earlier. It was empowering, and, for some, overwhelming. Many became emotional through the experience. Sometimes, those participants would say "You are so motivating!" I'm not going to lie, it felt good to hear, but in reality, I didn't do anything! They did the work! They pushed past barriers and overcame their preconceived limits! I wished instead they would have said, "I'm inspired realizing I can do more than I thought I was capable of!"

Because of their self-limiting beliefs, years of conditioning focused on surface-level outcomes, they failed to see that they were inspired based on their own experience! Motivation may have played a role in getting there, but the outcome, and what made it endure, was inspiration and the recognition that their own achievements inspired them.

Wayne Dyer, the now-passed author and teacher, defines motivation as "getting a hold of an idea and taking it to its logical conclusion, and not letting anything interfere," which applies to internal and external motivation. He continues: "If that is the definition of motivation, then the definition of Inspiration is the exact opposite! Inspiration is when an idea gets a hold of you and takes you where you were originally intended to go in the first place!"

The essay "Where madness is psyche's only nurse" demonstrates the idea with the following anecdote:

A young musician and future-composer once asked Mozart, "How do I write a symphony?" He was a little put off when Mozart replied, "You are still young, start by writing menuettos." The young musician said, "Well you were writing symphonies when you were younger than I!" To which Mozart replied from a place of humble honesty "Yes, but I did not ask anyone how to do it." The symphonies presented themselves to Mozart in such a powerful way he had no choice but to follow that inspiration. The young musician was motivated, but Mozart was Inspired!

When examining the root of the words, motivation and inspiration, a clearer distinction is observed. Inspiration comes from the root "From Spirit" and has religious and spiritual connotations, relating to the soul, source, or spirit within each of us. So "Inspiration" ultimately means alignment with the soul's highest purpose. Motivation's (motivate) earliest definition and association is the "act or process of furnishing with an incentive or inducement to action" – to act for incentive. The very roots of each word give clarity; *while motivation is tied to the outcome and achievement, inspiration is tied to intention, process, and purpose.*

To inspire is to allow choice and freedom. It might motivate someone to a higher level of performance by encouraging them with something like, "I know you have more!" But they would be responding for the wrong reason – to receive *the trainer's* praise. Inspiring someone to achieve a higher goal would be to ask, "What more do you have to give?" Or, as a former colleague frequently asked in her classes, "What can you do in 30 seconds!?"

Our focus should inspire us to give more; not acquire more!

Let's revisit the sales/motivation equation from earlier: current dissatisfaction + future promise > cost = fear. The industries that communicate this messaging and solutions expect consumers to accept their messages at face value. But what if, instead, each of us examined *WHY* we are dissatisfied, *WHY* we are looking for a brighter future, and *HOW* simple it is to overcome those hurdles to reach those unique future(s) through being inspired and inspiring ourselves and others.

If we are not passionately inspired to become the most authentic version of ourselves, eating and moving for all of the "right" reasons, our default is to try to live up to others' dreams, standards and expectations. And since others' expectations, solutions and paths are forever changing, we continue in vain to seek happiness, contentment and health conditional on the resulting outcomes.

How disheartening it is to do everything we've been told, work hard to achieve an outcome, only to realize the promised outcome is either unrealistic or doesn't deliver happiness. And then also to realize we didn't enjoy the process, and in many cases, sacrificed what was important to us, for something that seems important to someone else.

The more times we repeat the pattern, the further and further we find ourselves from where we want to be, because we don't really have clarity on where we want to be, who we want to be, why we want to be there, and how to *really* get there.

The truth is, we rarely consider the distinction between motivation and inspiration and how it can enhance or hinder our progress.

Patanjali, referred to by some as the "Father of Yoga," was a teacher nearly 2000 years ago. He taught Hindu scripture in a way that resonated with his followers using 'Sutras' and messages that are just as applicable today as they were 200 B.C. Of inspiration Patanjali said: *"When you're inspired by some great purpose, or extraordinary project, all your thoughts break their bonds. Your mind transcends limitations; your consciousness expands in every direction; and you find yourself in a new, great, and wonderful world. Dormant forces, faculties, and talents become alive. You discover yourself to be a greater person than you ever dreamed yourself to be!"*

We find that being authentically inspired in life is perhaps the very definition of Flow.

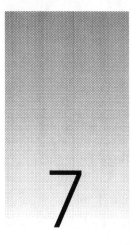

7

LIVING WITH INTENTION THROUGH CONTRAST: LIFE AS A "CONTINUUM"

A continuum is a scale that demonstrates an infinite number of points. The Wellness Continuum represents our infinite potential for progress.

After we are inspired to live the life we wish, we must take ownership of the actions and behaviors that will help us consistently progress in that direction.

I love to use a continuum to represent our progress toward the person we want to be; the most authentic and fully-expressed self, and provides some loose structural or procedural framework for some of these more abstract ideas, for analytical minds.

But perhaps we should define wellness first. I'm not crazy about any of the definitions I have found so I created my own for the purpose of illustrating this idea. Wellness is the collective whole, and interaction of, each of the individual parts, that make us each unique. Those 'parts' include things like physical health, mental and emotional health, intelligence, spirituality, social health and relationships, occupational and financial health, environmental factors etc.

We have done ourselves a huge disservice by placing more weight (no pun intended) on physical health, and then complicating it further by dumbing it down to using weight as the major metric of physical health and therefore a major wellness balance marker. Compounded further by only considering diet and exercise as the conditions that impact physical fitness and wellness.

The reality is that each individual domain of wellness will have both direct and indirect implications with the others. For example: Extra hours at work may lead to more financial gain, but also means more stress, and more stress may lead to irritability, which could show up in already strained relationships because of less time at home, or may influence our physical health because of sleep, food that we eat, and our exercise…

Finding balance within these areas is a life-long pursuit for each of us. Wellness is not an outcome, but a dynamic and constant process. Each individual component has implications to the other parts, and therefore the collective whole.

If we used a metric to rate our daily wellness at any given second, we would soon discover that the present wellness level is not guaranteed for any amount of time. Further, we discover that *each of our thoughts, behaviors, and actions throughout the day either move us closer to where we want to be, or further away from that optimal version of self.* Some have greater impacts than others, but quite literally everything we do is moving us to where we want to be, or away from that person.

And since none of the components of wellness are guaranteed, we also find that if we are not consciously aware, and intentionally moving forward with momentum toward who we wish to be, the default is not guaranteed or stationary, but instead unconsciously moving us away from that point.

A Good representation of this concept is looking at the global coronavirus pandemic. No one chose to lose access to their fitness centers, access to parks, access to certain food sources and shopping, social interaction etc.

And if we didn't create a conscious and purposeful plan to mitigate those factors that we didn't have control over, the result was looking in the mirror 12 months later and not recognizing the person looking back at us.

No one wakes up in the morning and asks themselves: "what can i do, eat, and think today that will make me sicker and further from my ideal self when I go to sleep tonight." But even without asking ourselves such a ridiculous question, if we aren't deliberately living, intentionally moving toward who we wish to be, that is exactly what we are unconsciously doing!

We also discover that it is usually not the big decisions, actions, and thoughts that have the greatest impact, but rather all the small, seemingly inconsequential ones, directing the momentum of life in one way or another. It's the little concessions that we give ourselves that go against our personal boundaries. It's our little justifications that dictate the actions that have the most impact in moving us further toward or away from where we hope to be.

Mentioned earlier in this book, but also feeling important to revisit here; a powerful "Why" is a prerequisite to recognize this concept. If we don't have an idea of "who we are" or "what the optimal self" is, it's difficult to navigate in that direction through our thoughts, actions, and behaviors.

We could all substantially improve our wellness and life experience if we were each more deliberate in our day-to-day lives in consistently asking ourselves "*Why* I am doing this?" and "will this move me closer to where I want to be?". That deliberateness over time will become habitual, and we will reach a place of enjoying the process because we aren't focused on someone else's predetermined goal or outcome.

Let's examine further this concept as it relates to the food we eat and how we move. If I choose to eat an Oreo cookie, it's not a decision that is going to have a big impact on my overall health one way or another. However, although not being 'significant' to overall health, we can observe that it's probably not moving me closer to my goal. If I chose to eat a sleeve of Oreos each day, it would be more impactful on my health, and if I ate two full packages each day: even more significant, and so on.

As discussed, everything we do and consume has effects on our wellness to different degrees. I believe soda pop is perhaps the single greatest contributing factor to our global health and obesity epidemic. When soda first was made available for public consumption and sale, it was a *treat* that people enjoyed in small quantities, and on a very infrequent basis. Today it's common for many sugar-addicted folks to consume hundreds of ounces every day. What was once an occasional treat without great impact, is now an accepted norm wreaking havoc on society's collective health.

We find the same association with movement and exercise. Every step we take, or don't take; every repetition of every exercise, is moving us to a healthier version of self, or further away. There are no guaranteed health outcomes for anyone! Our wellness is conditional on all our thoughts, actions, and behaviors, not just the ones we think matter.

Most of us fail to make the connection between the "little" things, regardless of them being the most impactful, albeit over time; and that's where we must acknowledge the problem originating. There is little need or desire for delayed gratification in the current "have everything now" mentality. Most of us make the decisions that dictate our lives from an "all-or-nothing" perspective with a focus on what we feel are "big-picture" items. Recognizing the impact of each of our actions and thoughts is not easy to acknowledge or recognize, partly due to our inclination toward all-or-nothing thinking patterns. We struggle seeing the forest for the trees. All-or-nothing thinking is regular, but conditioned, human response and common cognitive distortion in which we catastrophize the outcomes as opposite and usually extreme. Rather than viewing things as "grey area" or process, we opt for limited outcome-focus, and in black and white terms. This unhealthy thinking pattern is of greater impact because we have unwittingly and unnecessarily tied our food and movement to outcome, and in so doing have placed greater implications on what we do and don't do. We justify that "well I can't work out for more than 20 minutes so I might as well not do anything!" or "I already ate something I shouldn't have, so might as well wait to start again tomorrow" All-or-nothing thinking and actions fosters an environment that diminishes recognition of the impact(s) of our decisions, thoughts, and actions, encourages procrastination, and allows external forces to be motivation, and quantifiers of success and/or perceived failure. All-or-nothing thinking focuses on faults and negative self-defeating thoughts; instead of focusing on strengths, progress and the ability to recognize the positive in everything.

Tony Robbins is credited with saying: "It's not what we do once in a while that shapes our lives; it's what we do consistently." I agree with this observation of consistency, however, the purpose of this book is to not only recognize the impact of our daily thoughts, decisions and actions, but to also examine the intention behind those thoughts, decisions and actions.

Contrast

One way we learn through this intentional and purposeful approach is considering the contrasting points on any continuum or scale. Once again I found myself without a definition, I liked so I came up with my own. Contrast is the range between two opposite points on a scale. The greater the contrast, the greater the knowledge and experience to serve as future reference in our lives.

We understand that without our experience of pain, our appreciation of pleasure may be limited. Without sadness, we can't know joy etc. Perhaps less understood is how the range of contrast impacts our experience and lives. Carl Jung said: "The greater the contrast, the greater the potential. Great energy only comes from a correspondingly great tension of opposites."

This is especially important to consider with the concept of flow, living life in the path of least resistance. Let me explain; we traditionally view unfavorable events, traits, characteristics, etc. as "Bad". But those less-than-favorable experiences are what provide the frame of comparison, and as a result are ultimately positive. But it is more than just conceptually seeing the proverbial glass as "half full' vs "half empty.

American Spiritual Author Neil Donald Walshe provides a "Law of Attraction" interpretation of the role contrast plays as we create and live our lives. He taught: "as soon as we desire anything in life, we simultaneously manifest the opposite!" This seems to be a paradox and cause to question

How or Why that could be the case! In desiring anything, we are indirectly acknowledging that we are lacking that very thing, providing the contrast, and increasing desire of what we want.

As this is a book about body composition, let's examine this idea as it relates to body image, and self-esteem. We are better at observing thinking-errors in others than we are at observing them within ourselves. It isn't that we make judgments about ourselves, and don't judge others; but rather we judge ourselves much more harshly than others and hold ourselves to a higher standard (usually set by someone else) than others. So when a friend says something like "I need to lose weight" it is easy for us to see that that may or may not be the case, and whether true or not, we communicate words of support or affirmation. When we look at ourselves, and say the same thing: "I need to lose weight", we lack the grace for self that we often openly extend to others, and we may develop shame and guilt that only compounds the more we are unable to recognize the perfection within us as we presently are. We say things to and about ourselves that we wouldn't dream of uttering out loud to others or about others. Human nature seems to lead us to recognize and acknowledge all that we seemingly lack, rather than all that we already are. This discussion of Contrast can be applied to Flow.

Contrast and Flow

The commonly shared quote "When it Rains it Pours" represents the momentum of our thoughts, behaviors and actions. It's all around us. We witness others who we consider "positive" or happy, and it seems effortless for those to live in a constant state of joy, and why wouldn't they? They have *everything* (in our eyes)! Conversely, the opposite is also true. We view others whom we consider ornery or in a bad mood, and it appears just as effortless for those folks to remain in a state of indifference. In both circumstances, we are correct; it is effortless for both individuals.

We witness others who we deem "healthy" without even trying to be so, while we feel like we can never do enough to achieve that same level. And with that kind of thinking, we are right about that as well.

We are also familiar with the quote: "you are what you eat" which is partially true, but I would like to extend that thought one step further. "We are what we consume." It may not appear to be anything more than just a minor change in vernacular. But to "consume" is not limited to physical consumption of food!

Now the idea here is not just to point out the obvious and show that we are what we eat, or we become who we surround ourselves with etc. and attempt to force ourselves to be more accountable to those factors, be compelled to change our behaviors and actions, and push, work, and endure, until we reach an outcome. Instead, the idea is to view contrast and its momentum in a different way, based not on outcome, but by intentional living in the present.

Because of our culturally outcome-focused drive, we judge others and ourselves, instead of just observing, acknowledging, and allowing, factors that are oftentimes out of our control as just that, out of our control and therefore, should be out of our mind.

For example, if a person diets to lose weight, they usually have a number in mind of how many pounds they would like to lose. If they subsequently don't achieve that number, or if it takes longer than anticipated, it can lead to feelings of guilt and shame. As a result, the person says something like: "I failed at hitting my goal" or "I failed my diet" etc. Outcome focus requires a judgment; and that judgment is black and white. We either fail or succeed; there are no other options. The reality is that truth lies somewhere in the infinite, between those two clearly defined end points.

Let's use water to examine further. Imagine a vessel filled halfway with water. The water will adapt to the shape of the container and any external stimulus on that container. As the water adapts to the size, shape, and stimuli, we don't judge the water for behaving positively or negatively. The water isn't good or bad as it changes; it simply "is". The water "flows". Upon examining further water and its characteristics, another takeaway is the relationship between momentum and contrast. The greater the force upon the water, the greater the response of the water in the receptacle. If a pebble was dropped into the water, it may cause a small ripple that dissipates quickly, but with increasing size of rocks, also comes increasing size of splash and ripples. Through all of its adaptation, the volume of water does not change; instead, it flows in the state of constant adaptation to its environment.

Similarly, our lives consist of infinite factors. We control some, but the majority of what is going on around us is more about our response and adaptation, than it is about our attempting to force a specific outcome. Additionally new experiences with factors out of our control, expand our experience, knowledge, and ability to adapt to similar circumstances in the future. Our resiliency increases to a point that we acknowledge and find peace in the things we cannot control. Life shouldn't be about enduring to a result, but rather living in a state of Flow; or living with inspired intention.

The "To be or not to be" soliloquy from Shakespeare's Hamlet, is one the most famous pieces of prose in all of literature. The context of Hamlet's pontification is ultimately questioning whether living a life of struggle is worth living at all. I don't wish to challenge that meaning Shakespeare intended; however, I would love to use those same words in different contexts.

If we take the eastern philosophy of "to be" we could define it as something like: "living without judgment or attachment." To "Be" is to authentically flow in life through the path of least resistance. If we use that context of "Be" in regard to Hamlet's question, it provides a much different perspective., ultimately leading us to ask ourselves "to flow or not to flow," "to be inspired or not to be inspired" "to inspire or not inspire" or "to live intentionally, or to not live intentionally" We discover that our ability to Be, or to flow, is ultimately a choice within our power to create.

As we discover our flow-state(s), we begin to realize how much of our lives are based on conditions. As we release the conditions, we release the expectations and judgments associated with those conditional outcomes, and we discover another truth within ourselves shared simply and eloquently by Neale Donald Walsch: "Everything I have ever been, and everything I will ever be, I currently am."

8

MARLEY AND PEPPER (AN ALLEGORY)

Anyone who has been blessed to feel the unconditional love that only pets can provide, understands that they, like our children, are teaching us as much, if not more, than we are teaching them. I have two dogs, Pepper and Marley, who aside from the shared genes (Pepper is Marley's mom) and the entirety of their environment, couldn't be more different! Pepper is female, and Marley is male. Pepper is light in color with dark markings, while Marley is dark with light markings. Pepper is about 10 pounds lighter and 3 inches shorter than Marley. Pepper's preferred toy is a ball of any size or material, and Marley prefers soft, plush squeaky toys and the attention of people and other dogs. Pepper likes to be pet on her neck and back and is not very cuddly. Marley demands attention and whenever someone sits down, he positions himself immediately in front of them, and loves to flop and cuddle while getting his belly and ears scratched. Pepper prefers sleeping on smooth cool surfaces like the kitchen bathroom floor, while Marley likes sleeping on the soft bed.

During a recent visit to the dog-park I observed and recognized another behavioral difference between Marley and Pepper that made me question something else not previously considered, whether they are each living their fullest dog-life. When we arrive at the dog-park, both dogs are equally anxious to get inside, although the motivation seems to be very different.

Upon entering, Marley immediately spends the first few minutes running around to each dog, walking in circles and exchanging customary bottom-sniffing. After he's introduced himself to all the other dogs, he runs from person to person, allowing each to briefly say hello and scratch his head. After all the introductions have been made, Marley spends his time splashing in the water, and running around with the other dogs playing, jumping, chasing, pooping, sniffing, peeing, etc, only stopping these urgent activities when a new dog enters the park, and the process starts all over.

Pepper's behavior is very different. She enters the park and spends however long is necessary (although usually less than 30 seconds) looking for a tennis ball. She searches with such intensity that her body often shakes with excitement and anticipation of the fun the ball will provide. A ball for Pepper is a prerequisite or requirement for fun and it's literally all that matters to her in that moment. (Marley enjoys playing with, and chasing, tennis balls and playing fetch too, however it doesn't seem to be nearly as important or required for the fun.) Once Pepper has found "her" ball she will be the only dog that touches that ball while at the park. She is very fast and understands how I throw the ball and how the ball will react with the ground, ensuring that she will always be the first dog to reach it. When she is not retrieving the ball, she lays down or sits down with the ball 6 inches in front of her with her eyes glued on it with complete focus. When other dogs come close to introduce themselves or try to sniff her, she growls and flashes her teeth in perceived defense of her prized possession. I am the only person she allows to pick up her ball, and I'm sure it's only because she understands that the few seconds it is in my care is in preparation for her increased pleasure. If I hold it too long, she barks her disapproval. If I pretend to throw it and fake her out, she barks for attention, ensuring that I observe that she is sitting "patiently" although her body is shaking in anticipation. At the dog park, the tennis ball is Pepper's whole existence. She does not have any interest in other dogs or people.

I've been reflecting about my dogs' behavior, and it's led me to deeper philosophical questions for myself. Which dog is living the more fun and full life? Should either of them be trained to be different? Should we embrace or condemn any of the behaviors as not appropriate for a dog?

Marley's easy-going, playful personality allows living in the moment without the condition of another dog or toy or anything else. He's open and curious and allows new exposure and new experiences. Marley lives for the present without thought of past or future. Pepper has made the decision for herself that a ball is, and will always be, the greatest source of joy, and is unwilling to even consider an alternative.

Is Pepper's obsession with a ball "good" or "bad" as it relates to her enjoyment and experience? One could argue that such focus on the ball is a distraction preventing her from experiencing so much more! Or one could also argue that her focus and intention allows her to create her fullest life. Of course, we are talking about dogs, and human behaviors are different. And a more human response, would not be so black and white. It would be great if the dogs had the capacity to acknowledge "I can't think of anything that would make me happier than playing with this ball, but I'm open and curious to consider another option."

Obviously, there are some clear distinctions between dogs and people; and I don't think many people live like either of my dogs. I don't know too many people as carefree as Marley, and I don't know anyone so focused on isolated and external sources of joy as Pepper. However, I have observed in myself and others when I have exhibited these traits and patterns. Looking at their experiences, I can ask myself: Which dog is living the fuller life?

Which dog's behavior do I identify with more? And what does this tell me about where I am at, what I value, and what I want?

What "tennis balls" in my life are distracting my attention from something greater? (What things am I settling for right now to avoid things from my past preventing me from authentically showing up in the present?)

One thing we discover in asking ourselves these questions, is that there isn't a "right" or "wrong" answer. We all get to answer the questions for ourselves, and those answers are "correct/right" for us, and regardless of the answer, we can find a place of peace and acceptance there, independent of anyone or anything else. We MUST start from that place of self-acceptance and love in where we are right now if we intend on consistent flowing forward momentum.

As we each allow the processing and unfolding in this process of self-discovery, we can consider other dialectic concepts using the same continuum framework to assist each of us in determining our purpose and path(s).

9

SAFETY, RISK, AND REWARD

Let's begin by examining the balance of the contrasting ideas of safety and risk as they relate to reward. I would rather use "progress" instead of "reward" because 'progress' is process and isn't limited by the same conditions as 'rewards' which is outcome-driven. That said, we will use the more common "reward" for our discussion, understanding that the reward is representative of progress.

If we once again view our life as a continuum; one direction is safety, and the other direction is the risk. Where we each find ourselves on that scale in relationship to previous points, is the metric of progress reward.

Before talking about the correlations, it's important to define these key concepts. In speaking of "Safety" here, we are talking about "emotional safety." In psychology, emotional safety is a condition that is achieved regarding attachment theory, where each contributor is open and vulnerable. Perhaps it is because we associate emotional safety with attachment that we rarely even consider emotional safety within ourselves, because most are not considering their attachment or connection to self as of equal or greater importance than attachment to another person, whether healthy or unhealthy. It's much more difficult to identify healthy or unhealthy attachment to self (ego) than in our relationships with others. Additionally, we usually prioritize our attachment behaviors and how they may impact our relationships with others more, and with higher intensity, then we ever do in looking at our relationship with self.

Risk and Reward have their own definitions. Risk means there's a possibility of some type of trial, harm or damage, and reward is any recognition of effort or achievement. For the sake of discussion here, we will discuss their relationship to each other first, and then how that risk/reward balance relates to, and is influenced by, safety.

The Risk-Reward paradigm is one that most of us are familiar with. The risk-reward tradeoff states that the potential reward/outcome rises with an increase in risk. Using this principle, individuals associate low levels of uncertainty with low rewards and high levels of risk with potentially higher rewards.

In looking at the delicate balance between these two seemingly contrasting concepts of safety, risk, and reward, we observe that regarding autonomy of self, when speaking of "safety" humans are more conditioned to seek safety externally, while when considering "risk" as how it will impact them internally or personally! If we really want to find balance in safety and risk, and progress to the person we wish to be, we must start by observing and considering safety and risk from the same vantage point, because any other option feeds external validation, external accountability, or external motivation.

When examining it closer, or viewing the paradigm in different light, we observe more. We find that the conditions, extent, and limitations of safety and reward are conditional on the unknown, vulnerability, or risk. With very little risk, there is little reward, but there is also limited emotional safety. The greater the vulnerability of risk and the unknown expanse, the greater the reward in living authentically to our purpose, AND more importantly, the greater the foundation of and range of emotional safety we feel in becoming the person we wish to become.

10

CONDITIONAL VS UNCONDITIONAL

There seems to be a spiritual awakening (for lack of a better name) in humanity right now toward authenticity and personal growth. A concept regularly discussed is that of conditional and unconditional love. And similar to the Safety/Risk/Reward paradigm, our thoughts in regard to conditional vs unconditional love are often misdirected; or at least we focus more energy and attention on the love we feel for others more than recognizing the foundational need of love to be for self. Many of us don't realize that love does not have to be received externally! We seek love from others to "feel" love; and in many cases we may even sacrifice who we are, our values, and what we want in order to appease others because receiving love feels so good! Is there anything wrong with feeling, receiving, or sharing love with others; whether conditional or unconditional? Certainly not, but what if our capacity to give and receive love didn't require another person? What if we could feel love at the same intensity within ourselves? What if we could love ourselves as much as we have ever loved another? Many reading this will say "of course" as if it is the obvious and only answer. Others would reply to the opposite "No way!" with just as much certainty. Both groups can be "right" based on their unique experience(s) with love based on our familial, cultural, and societal experiences.

However, isn't the requirement of another person to love (or be loved by) a condition? If another person (with their own actions, behaviors, thoughts, values, needs etc.) is a "condition" Is it even possible to unconditionally love another person? Many will say "I love my children unconditionally" but even in that seemingly obvious example, it shows us that the child(ren) are conditions to directing that love!

If we consider that other people are "conditions," we also gain clarity that love of self is really the only literal "unconditional" love. Ironically, we are hardest on ourselves, and have the most conditions for ourselves that dictate how much love we feel for ourselves. We say things to ourselves that we would never dream of telling another. We judge ourselves more harshly than anyone else. We create our own self-limiting beliefs, and then reinforce them with the external conditions in which we live, that then dictate our decisions, actions and thoughts.

What if something as simple as self-acceptance or self-love is the key? What if we saw ourselves for the perfect person, we each are, in every moment? What if we stopped comparing ourselves to others? What if we stopped chasing others' dreams and expectations? What if it was all as simple as being able to look in the mirror, into our own eyes, and telling ourselves "I love me" and meaning it enough to feel the authenticity of those words?

It is not only that simple, but it's also a requirement if we are seeking the change within, and grow into who we wish to become. Additionally, no system of diet, exercise, therapy, etc. will get us to that self-actualized version of being, without first having a deep connection to self, based on love for everything we (already) are, and grace for our (perceived) shortcomings, or weaknesses. A favorite meditation mantra of mine is: "When I love myself, loving others is easy." We must unconditionally love ourselves because our self is the only real source of unconditional love.

RADICAL ACCOUNTABILITY

"Accountability" is a common concept within systems and programs of self-improvement. Typically, it is discussed in terms of 'internal' and 'external,' (which we will also discuss), but to begin the discussion, suffice to say that we, humans, love accountability; but mostly for others. We also find that we aren't too great with personal or internal accountability, and don't have the same degree of engagement when we are being held accountable by others.

Human beings are great at pointing out why others' behavior requires them to be held accountable for their actions and behaviors, many times simply because they see things differently than us. We demand accountability for others, while at the same time justifying our own behaviors that those around us would hold us similarly accountable for.

Following the usage of the continuum conceptual framework, if one direction on the scale represents accountability, the opposite direction, is justification.

There are many definitions of "Accountability" but my favorite comes from Brene Brown who defined it as "owning mistakes, apologizing, and making amends." I like the definition because the opposite end of "justification" is veiled behind "owning" our mistakes. There is a lot of shame around our actions we perceive as mistakes or wrongdoing by ourselves and others. We make excuses for our behavior because we feel guilt and shame. But what if we allowed grace for ourselves enough to recognize that we are not perfect, and we do things that others would not understand and like, AND at the same time be okay with that.

I am not saying that there aren't times I feel other's should be held accountable; there most definitely are. More important would be our ability to recognize how much of our energy we are giving to something that we have no control over, and in many cases are guilty of the same. This is where radical accountability comes into play, not as a vehicle of personal guilt or shame, but rather a vehicle for growth, progress, and connection. There always have been, and will continue to be, things that are both in and out of our personal control. Radical accountability is the idea that regardless of our individual control of circumstances; our responses, actions/reactions, should ultimately be the same. Initially the concept may be difficult to process, until we recognize all the ways the concept already permeates our day-to-day lives. An example of this is the commonly shared Serenity Prayer: "Grant me the serenity to accept the things I cannot change, the courage to change the things I can, and the wisdom to know the difference." When we examine the prayer's words more closely, we find that serenity, courage, and wisdom are not innate characteristics, but rather the result of repetitive intentional and purposeful thoughts, decisions, and actions. Serenity is the foundation of acceptance and accountability. Without that foundation, we can forget about developing courage to change the things we control, or the wisdom to know the difference; and as a result, get caught up and bogged down in a state of victimhood.

Not only is radical accountability the baseline for growth, but the opposite is also futile and frustrating. We can't control others' behaviors, thoughts, or actions, and any attempt to do so usually results in discord and contention, and further separation. We find this scenario in most current human interactions: relationships, religious dogmatism, political fanaticism, sports and even work. Instead of approaching the uncontrollable circumstances in our lives from a place of learning, we approach them on guard. Instead of recognizing that we are really on the same team, in nearly every interaction we are either playing offense or defense. The solution isn't simply radical acceptance, but acceptance must certainly be foundational in the process if the intention is growth and progress.

When we are approached with uncontrollable circumstances, radical accountability is the ability to ask ourselves: What is my responsibility here? Am I guilty of the same thing that I'm observing in others? What can I do to make this better for myself and others? What could have I done differently? How could I have responded differently? What can I learn from my emotional response to the circumstance? How will I respond differently next time?

These are the questions that can provide perspective with others and if/how we allow circumstances to affect our behavior, and ultimately lead to the internal questions that allow us to discover the autonomy of our authentic self.

Radical accountability is not blind acceptance of the injustices we see and have experienced, but rather the ability to identify our part, and create solutions that are in alignment with our values, path, and desired outcomes. It is about what we each can do. It's about the factors we can control. It's acknowledging our power to create and live the life we want. Ultimately, it's about loving ourselves unconditionally.

12

AUTONOMY AND AUTHENTICITY
IN SELF-LOVE

Unconditional self-love is not easy; not because it's unnatural, but instead because we have been taught to look for love and validation outside of ourselves. When we strip down all the layers of the external expectations, conditions, and patterns; what is left is the authentic self. Discovering this version of ourselves can be scary, because we may not like what we see. We may not like how we feel. We may realize that we have spent the majority of our lives inauthentically, for others. If we wish to live differently, we must first do the work to know who we are. We must look at our own skeletons in the closet, we must look at the parts of ourselves that make us unique without judgment or comparison.

"Character" has been defined as what one does when no one is looking. I would like to take it an extra step deeper. Our character is not only what we do when no one is looking, but also what we think about in the privacy of our own thoughts.

More importantly than our character, observed by thoughts and actions, is examining "why" those are our thoughts and actions. Observing and acknowledging the intention behind the thoughts and actions can be difficult because we've spent most of our lives allowing external sources to determine what our "Why(s)" should be.

Psychologists collectively believe that each person navigates day-to-day living as two different versions of self. The public self is the version we wish others to see; and it takes a conscious and intentional effort to portray. Our private self is made up of the things that we wish to hide from those around us, in an attempt to keep it hidden. Our authentic self is made up of traits and characteristics of each of these versions of self. Perhaps more important than knowing the differences in these versions of self, is once again being able to identify "why" we are showing up differently with different people and in different circumstances.

In recognizing that we all have different versions of self, allows us to see that others are only allowing us to see the versions of themselves that they wish to be. So, when we assess others' character, we often confuse the versions, and as a result may make snap-judgments. The traditional interpersonal model of two (or more) individuals meeting or coming together to connect in some capacity is inauthentic from the get-go, and as a result open the door for relationship and connection dilemmas. The judgments we make about others or circumstances are then often unfounded. And other assumptions about us are also unfounded and many times limiting. We see this dilemma play out similarly in nearly every part of our lives and our interactions with others. Social media, politics, work environment, dating (online dating is even more obvious) etc.

We are more comfortable living our lives externally to be loved, accepted and validated by others, so we change our behavior to align with those outcomes.

We attempt to force connection with others based on inauthenticity in both parties leading to shallow connection, rather than finding love and alignment in self and allowing others to flow in and out of our lives based on who we really are.

The great basketball coach John Wooden is credited with saying: "Pay more mind to your character than your reputation; because your character is who you really are; while your reputation is merely who others think you are."

Sometimes, we attempt to convince ourselves that we are someone we are not without even knowing it! We want connection, acceptance and validation so much that we perform mental gymnastics convincing ourselves that our values and wants are different than they are. So, we find dishonesty is just as prevalent with ourselves as it is observable in others.

Do we treat different people or groups differently? Do we show up differently in our relationships with different people? Is our personal and professional persona the same? Are there things in our lives that we hide from others? Are there things about our thoughts, behaviors and actions that we feel guilt or shame about? Would the story of our life be the same in a hypothetical scenario where each of our thoughts, behaviors, actions, habits, words, interactions etc. were broadcast to the world? I don't know if it is possible to live with that level of external authenticity, and in observing the answers to these questions within ourselves, we find that we are each, to some degree, attempting to control the narrative of our lives as observable to others.

The answers to these questions; the things we choose not to let others see, are our shadows. If our goal is to live an autonomous, authentic, and fully expressed life, we have to come to peace with these parts of who we are; and we have to recognize them and embrace them for the part they have played in making us who we are. We must accept them from a place of love for self as strength and uniqueness, instead of recoiling and burying them in layers of conditioned guilt and shame.

That said, behaviors and actions alone are not indicative of authenticity. We can observe two different people doing the same thing, but for very different reasons; and so we find that character and authenticity are more closely tied to intention than behavior. An example of this is giving to charity. The action of giving to charity is seemingly positive or "good" but the intention may vary. One may give of themselves in order to receive personal gain like a tax benefit, or to be observed by others for recognition as a "good person" who contributes to others' health and safety. Others give independent of any other person's knowledge. In both circumstances, both individuals are doing something good; but that does not mean that each of them is operating out of authenticity. They may be but they also may not. Just like we are the only ones capable of unconditional love for ourselves, only we individually know the truth of what is motivating our decisions and actions. CS Lewis said of "integrity" what I feel can be applied to authenticity: "Integrity involves doing the right thing, even when no one is watching" Similarly I once heard someone say: "Everything you need to know about a person can be observed by what they do with their shopping cart in the parking lot after unloading groceries."

It is important to acknowledge the correlation between authenticity and unconditional self-love. Do we really accept and love all of who we are (shadows and closet-skeletons included), or are we projecting externally that we unconditionally love ourselves for others to observe?

In examining the depths of authenticity, observing intention, behaviors, thoughts, actions, talents, and skeletons etc., we may need a push and guidance to dig a little deeper, which is uncomfortable and necessary, and serves as the content of Part 2 of this book.

PART 2

PIIP CONCEPTUAL FRAMEWORK

13

PUTTING IT ALL TOGETHER!

After peeling back the layers of self-limiting doubt, expectations, conditions, processes and systems; we begin to realize the power we each hold to create the uniquely beautiful and authentic life we each want! I want to introduce the following conceptual model and some associated exercises to assist us each in finding our authentic purpose and ensure that we are living in alignment toward that progress with momentum, and without resistance.

This model is a four-circle Venn diagram. The four circles are "Purpose" "Intention" "Inspiration" and "Process" and the section/portion of the diagram where all four sections cross and intersect is our self-actualized and authentic self.

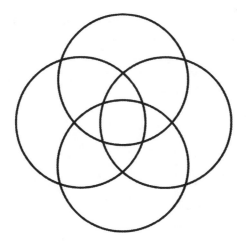

The four rings provide clarity through their associated questions and answers. The questions may feel cliche, but their answers can take a life to acknowledge and define. The questions, and their answers, are more important than the rings themself. Maybe not more important, but clarifies and gives direction, specific to process instead of outcome.

Each of the four sections have a question associated allowing us to reflect and dig deeper.

The question associated with "Purpose" is "Who Am I?".

The question tied to "Intention" is "Who do I want to be?" (Not to be confused with the unintentional and conditioned question: "who do I want others to think I am?" although if the answers to these questions are contrasting, that information and interpretation is telling.)

The question for the "Inspiration" section is "Why do I want to be that versions of self?" (Referring to the "Intention" answer from above.)

And the question(s) associated with "Process" are the systems and programs of "Hows" in regard to how we live.

Because we live in the conditioned society introduced and discussed earlier in chapter 2, we are told who we should be and what our purposes are, instead of asking and discovering ourselves. And since we are told who we should be, we are also directed how to get there! Instead of allowing the "process" to be the organic and authentic fruition of simply "living life;" we are told the way(s) is/are systems and programs of diets and exercise programs to a desired outcome.

14

PURPOSE

**The top ring represents "purpose." And
answers the question "Who am I?"**

Let us start with the most obvious question, which just so happens to be
one of the most deep philosophical questions one could hope to answer in
life: "Who Am I?"

As humans, we think we know who we are, or more accurately we think
we know who we should be. Much of who we think we are, and who we
think we should be is based on conditioning and conditions, expectations,
tangible metrics, quantifiable components etc. In many circumstances we

tie our "value" and "values" to those same tangible, physical and quantifiable outcomes, rather than the unconditional acceptance that we are already exactly who we are, and that we don't *need* to be anything or anyone else!

As mentioned, defining our purpose is a lifelong commitment of intention, but acknowledgement of our core values serves as the foundation of all other growth within this model of self-actualization.

Use the template or a separate sheet of paper to complete the following activity: Write 10 "I am" statements using "values" that you recognize are part of you. Allow grace for yourself; and instead of being critical for the things you aren't, list with pride all that you are! They should be perceived as positive values to you, but the key is that you must really believe in the value association with who you authentically are; and if you must "fake it til you make it" at least write values that you can defend yourself for having, even if your self-concept doesn't actually believe it; yet.

If you are struggling with identifying 10 values, please review the list to provide more scope and depth of character and individuality.

Examples of Values

Abundant	Compassionate	Stewardship
Accepted	Competent	Strong
Accomplished	Confident	Structured
Accountable	Consistent	Successful
Accurate	Content	Supportive
Achieved	Contributing	Surprising
Adaptive	Control	Sustainable
Adventurous	Cooperative	Teamwork
Affectionate	Courageous	Temperance
Alert	Courteous	Thankful
Ambitious	Creative	Thorough
Assertive	Credible	Thoughtful
Attentive	Curios	Timely
Authentic	Decisive	Tolerant
Aware	Rigorous	Tough
Balanced	Secure	Traditional
Beautiful	Self-actualized	Tranquil
Bold	Self-developed	Transparent
Brave	Self-reliant	Trustworthy
Brilliant	Self-respected	Understanding
Calm	Selfless	Unique
Capable	Sensitive	Unifying
Careful	Serene	Vision
Caring	Service	Vitality
Certain	Sharing	Wealthy
Challenged	Silence	Welcoming
Charitable	Simplicity	Winning
Clean	Sincere	Wise
Clear	Skillful	Dedicated
Clever	Solitary	Dependable
Comfortable	Speed	Determined
Committed	Spiritual	Devoted
Communicating	Stabile	Dignified
Community	Status	Disciplined

Diverse	Health	Organization
Efficient	Honesty	Originality
Empathic	Honor	Passion
Enduring	Humility	Patience
Energetic	Humor	Patriotism
Enjoyment	Imagination	Peace
Enthusiastic	Independence	Playfulness
Equality	Individuality	Poise
Ethical	Inner	Positivity
Excellence	Harmony	Power
Excited	Innovation	Productivity
Experienced	Insightful	Professional
Expert	Inspiring	Prosperity
Exploration	Integrity	Purpose
Fair	Intelligence	Quality
Faithful	Intuitive	Recognition
Fame	Joy	Respect
Family	Justice	Responsibility
Fearless	Kindness	Restraint
Fidelity	Knowledge	Results-oriented
Fit	Lawful	
Focused	Leadership	
Foresight	Learning	
Forgiveness	Logic	
Freedom	Love	
Friendship	Loyalty	
Fun	Mastery	
Generosity	Maturity	
Giving	Meaning	
Goodness	Moderation	
Grace	Motivation	
Gratitude	Obedience	
Growth	Openness	
Happiness	Optimism	
Hard Work	Order	
Harmony		

Complete the following 10 statements with your values!

I am _____!

I am _____!

I am _____!

I am _____!

I am _____!

I am _____!

I am _____!

I am _____!

I am _____!

I am _____!

For each of the 10 Values listed above in the "I am" statements, briefly describe what that value means to you and how you identify that value in your life.

* _____
_____
_____

* _____
_____
_____

* _____
_____
_____

* _____
_____
_____

* _____
_____
_____

* _____
_____
_____

* _____
_____
_____

* _____
_____
_____

*

_____

_____

_____

*

_____

_____

_____

*

_____

_____

_____

*

_____

_____

_____

*

_____

_____

_____

*

_____

_____

_____

*

_____

_____

_____

*

_____

_____

_____

*

_____

_____

_____

15

INTENTION

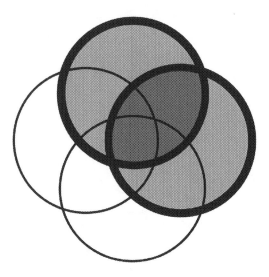

**The right ring represents "Intention." And answers
the question "Who do I want to be?"**

After the initial process of discovery in regard to who we are and have
identified the values, we hold that make us each uniquely who we are; the
next step toward self-actualization is to recognize who we want to be; or
identify the values we would like to identify with, even if we aren't quite there
yet. Important to note here is that none of who we want to be, diminishes
any or all of who we already are! We aren't attempting to trade one value
for another; so identifying those traits and values we perceive to be outside

of ourselves do not stem from scarcity or lack, but rather abundance and acceptance that we are powerful! We are in control of the lives we have lived, the lives we are living, and as a natural succession or result, the lives we wish to live to make up our future(s).

Identifying "who we want to be" can be an even more daunting and uncomfortable task than seeing who we really are; not because the desire is not there, but rather due to our upbringing and backgrounds, cultural and societal structures, family dynamics, and much more. Most of who we want to be is determined externally, and within those external constructs, we are taught which values are most important to our communities and families, and so we adapt to adopt those characteristics, even if we authentically don't really care about them. If they were really values that we "wished" or "intended" to have, we wouldn't have to convince ourselves to practice and live them; but rather they would already be parts of who we are, that we would be able to recognize and identify them in who we are!

Additionally in completing the following exercise, we begin to discover that many of the values we seek to obtain, are already within us, but we struggle to identify in some way or for some reason. The great teacher Rumi understood this simple concept by saying "The beauty you see in me, is a reflection of you." Due to cultural and societal conditioning, it is easier for us to see flaws in ourselves more than in others, and easier to observe good in others than ourselves.

These are not black and white concepts, and as organized graphically, some of the values listed in the "Purpose" activity, could be the same in this "Intention" activity.

Complete the following ten statements by filling in blank with a "value" you observe in others or want to develop.

I admire and would like to develop _____!

I admire and would like to develop _____!

I admire and would like to develop _____!

I admire and would like to develop _____!

I admire and would like to develop _____!

I admire and would like to develop _____!

I admire and would like to develop _____!

I admire and would like to develop _____!

I admire and would like to develop _____!

I admire and would like to develop _____!

For each of the ten values listed above (in which you would like to cultivate, develop and /or improve) write how your life will be once those traits are observable by self.

* _____
_____
_____
_____

* _____
_____
_____
_____

* _____
_____
_____
_____

* _____
_____
_____
_____

* _____
_____
_____
_____

* _____
_____
_____
_____

* _____
_____
_____
_____

* _____
_____
_____
_____

Jared Jones

* _____
_____
_____

* _____
_____
_____

* _____
_____
_____

* _____
_____
_____

* _____
_____
_____

* _____
_____
_____

* _____
_____
_____

* _____
_____
_____

* _____
_____
_____

16

INSPIRATION AND EMOTION RECOGNITION

The left ring represents "Emotion and Inspiration." And answers the question "Why do I want to be *that* person?"

Once we have each done the personal and self-reflective work to identify "who we are" and "who we want to be" comes an increasingly transformative and impactful phase, identifying the beliefs behind the values. We get to observe not just the behaviors, actions and decisions that dictate our lives and circumstances, but also examine the intention and beliefs behind those actions and behaviors.

This section is the most transformative because as humans we rarely question the intention behind our behaviors. We are quick to notice and judge things in others, while remaining blind to the fact that we share many of the same characteristics that we see and fault in others. We live in such a state of programming, and we rarely even question our own behaviors or actions, let alone their intention(s); so much so that we will often defend our position with much greater intensity than we even care to invest ourselves in.

In order to understand this most transformative step, we must start by forgetting outcomes, programs, systems, expectations, analytics, metrics, etc. and we must start from a place within. We must look to our bodies for their perfect, yet very misunderstood, emotional communication systems.

Emotions are our bodies' ways of telling us something. We feel a certain way due to circumstance, and we respond to that in a way that feels natural. Real growth and expansion start when we consider not only our actions or our emotional responses, but also acknowledging, recognizing, and understanding *why* we are experiencing certain emotions. Then allowing that deeper understanding to direct our lives.

Through the repetition of life, we experience a wide range of emotions, as well as many responses to those emotions. As we experience similar responses to similar emotions, the responses become almost automatic or robotic in nature. What if we spent more time and energy on acknowledging the emotion we are experiencing, AND allow time and space to try to understand why we are feeling that way, in order to make the best choice? Viktor Frankl said "between stimulus and response there is space. In that space is our power to choose our response. In our response lies our growth and freedom." If we live patterned lives made of repeated behaviors, habits, and actions, we will continue to experience the same repeated emotional responses, and those limited responses prevent our personal growth and freedom to create the lives we desire.

Additionally, living lives of patterned habits exposes us to the same emotions, in all the same ways. As a result we experience the same few emotions through a wider spectrum of intensities, with little control over their polarized outward responding behaviors and actions, rather than allowing ourselves to identify different emotions that may lead to discovering something new. Further, without recognizing the import and impact of our emotional responses, we "dumb-down" our experience and oversimplify emotions to generally positive emotions like happiness, excitement, joy, calmness, contentment, and love, and generally negative emotions like sadness, anger, fear, guilt, shame, etc. In reality the spectrum of human emotion is diverse and dynamic, and so it's imperative to recognize the vast contrast in emotions if we intend to continue to progress and expand our understanding and experience.

Use the following list as a reference to review the diversity of the human emotional experience, as well as reference for the following activity. As you review the following emotions, differentiate them as either generally 'positive' or 'negative' by circling or highlighting one group to differentiate the groups.

acceptance	apathy	careless
admiration	apprehension	caring
adoration	arrogant	charity
affection	assertive	cheeky
afraid	astonished	cheerfulness
agitation	attentiveness	claustrophobic
agony	attraction	coercive
aggressive	aversion	comfortable
alarm	awe	confident
alarmed	baffled	confusion
alienation	bewildered	contempt
amazement	bitter	content
ambivalence	bitter sweetness	courage
amusement	bliss	cowardly
anger	bored	cruelty
anguish	brazen	curiosity
annoyed	brooding	cynicism
anticipating	calm	dazed
anxious	carefree	dejection

delighted	enthusiasm	hurt
demoralized	envy	hysteria
depressed	epiphany	idleness
desire	euphoria	impatient
despair	exasperated	indifference
determined	excitement	indignant
disappointment	expectancy	infatuation
disbelief	fascination	infuriated
discombobulated	fear	insecurity
discomfort	flakey	insightful
discontentment	focused	insulted
disgruntled	fondness	interest
disgust	friendliness	intrigued
disheartened	fright	irritated
dislike	frustrated	isolated
dismay	fury	jealousy
disoriented	glee	joviality
dispirited	gloomy	joy
displeasure	glumness	jubilation
distraction	gratitude	kind
distress	greed	lazy
disturbed	grief	liking
dominant	grouchiness	loathing
doubt	grumpiness	lonely
dread	guilt	longing
driven	happiness	loopy
dumbstruck	hate	love
eagerness	hatred	lust
ecstasy	helpless	mad
elation	homesickness	melancholy
embarrassment	hope	miserable
empathy	hopeless	miserliness
enchanted	horrified	mixed up
enjoyment	hospitable	modesty
enlightened	humiliation	moody
ennui	humility	mortified

mystified	relieved	suffering
nasty	reluctant	sullenness
nauseated	remorse	surprise
negative	resentment	suspense
neglect	resignation	suspicious
nervous	restlessness	sympathy
nostalgic	revulsion	tenderness
numb	ruthless	tension
obstinate	sadness	terror
offended	satisfaction	thankfulness
optimistic	scared	thrilled
outrage	schadenfreude	tired
overwhelmed	scorn	tolerance
panicked	self-caring	torment
paranoid	self-compassionate	triumphant
passion	self-confident	troubled
patience	self-conscious	trust
pensiveness	self-critical	uncertainty
perplexed	self-loathing	undermined
persevering	self-motivated	uneasiness
pessimism	self-pity	unhappy
pity	self-respecting	unnerved
pleased	self-understanding	unsettled
pleasure	sentimentality	unsure
politeness	serenity	upset
positive	shame	vengeful
possessive	shameless	vicious
powerless	shocked	vigilance
pride	smug	vulnerable
puzzled	sorrow	weak
rage	spite	woe
rash	stressed	worried
rattled	strong	worthy
regret	stubborn	wrath
rejected	stuck	
relaxed	submissive	

Now that we have reviewed a comprehensive list of emotions and familiarized ourselves with others, we can more easily identify the impact that our emotions have on our lives, and how much unconscious correlation there is between our emotions and our thoughts, behaviors and actions.

The first exercise is to help us discover the compounded impacts of our negative emotional responses, and what we may learn from them. Looking at the list of emotions above, select five that you classified as "negative" choosing the five you are most familiar with.

EXPLORING NEGATIVE EMOTIONS

Select and write down 5 'negative' emotions.

1. _____

2. _____

3. _____

4. _____

5. _____

For each of the selected negative emotions, briefly describe your experience of them. Include *where* you experience them. Include *when* you experience them, both in circumstance, frequency and duration. Describe *how* you experience them, in physical sensations, thoughts etc. Describe how your experience of them influences your behavior, actions, habits, thoughts etc.

1. _____

_____
_____
_____
_____
_____
_____
_____
_____
_____
_____
_____
_____
_____

Jared Jones

2. _____
_____
_____
_____
_____
_____
_____
_____
_____
_____
_____
_____
_____
_____
_____
_____

3. _____
_____
_____
_____
_____
_____
_____
_____
_____
_____
_____
_____
_____
_____
_____
_____
_____

4. _____

_____

_____

_____

_____

_____

_____

_____

_____

_____

_____

_____

_____

_____

_____

_____

5. _____

_____

_____

_____

_____

_____

_____

_____

_____

_____

_____

_____

_____

_____

_____

_____

_____

After reflecting on the negative emotions in our lives and examining when, where, and how we experience them, we reach the most pivotal question of *why* we are experiencing them the way we are.

Humans are hardwired to seek joy. We all want to be happy. We are in control of our emotional responses. If we have evolved to gravitate toward happiness, and we have control over our emotional responses, we recognize that choosing anything except joy, is also a choice. Why would we choose to be anything else? The only answer can be we are not aware that we are in control of our emotions, and we have been conditioned to a victim-mentality in a comparison society, leading us to believe that others create the standard of happiness, and if we don't or can't find happiness in the same ways, we are "less than." We allow others opinions and cultural constructs start to place self-limiting doubts into our minds about who we should be, and what emotions are acceptable and which ones are not. Society has created the perfect wellness storm then stigmatizes any person or group that doesn't fall in line, or that asks questions. The following activity allows us to dig a little deeper into our negative emotional experiences and will serve as foundational contrast to then evaluate our positive emotions and their associated responses.

EXPLORING NEGATIVE EMOTIONS (CONTINUED)

Taking into consideration and reflecting on the 5 negative emotions listed previously, as well as the descriptive personal experience of each; contemplate and write down any belief(s) you have in association with the negative emotional response. After identifying the belief, negative thought pattern, thinking error, etc, identify how it came into your experience. Is the story you are telling yourself true? Where did it originate?

1. _____

_____

_____

_____

_____

_____

_____

_____

_____

_____

2. _____

_____

_____

_____

_____

_____

_____

_____

_____

_____

_____

Jared Jones

3. _____
_____
_____
_____
_____
_____
_____
_____
_____
_____

4. _____
_____
_____
_____
_____
_____
_____
_____
_____
_____

5. _____
_____
_____
_____
_____
_____
_____
_____
_____
_____

After going through the previous exercises of exploration, we each discover that our negative emotional responses are false beliefs, stories we create, and in almost every circumstance and scenario are fear-based. We start to see our part in creating those fear-based scenarios, negative emotional responses etc.; but more importantly we discover that if we are the creators of our negative emotional responses, we must also have control over our positive emotional responses, and that we create the good, progress, and abundance in our lives in the same way that we allow negative emotional responses.

In order to reveal the contrast and emotional range within each of us, let's repeat similar activities and exercises for our motivating and positive emotions and emotional responses.

EXPLORING POSITIVE EMOTIONS

Select and write down 5 'positive' emotions.

1. _____

2. _____

3. _____

4. _____

5. _____

For each of the selected positive emotions, briefly describe your experience of them. Include *where* you experience them. Include *when* you experience them, both in circumstance, frequency and duration. Describe *how* you experience them, in physical sensations, thoughts etc. Describe how your experience of them influences your behavior, actions, habits, thoughts etc.

1. _____

_____

_____

_____

_____

_____

_____

_____

_____

_____

_____

_____

_____

2. _____

_____
_____
_____
_____
_____
_____
_____
_____
_____
_____
_____
_____
_____
_____
_____
_____

3. _____

_____
_____
_____
_____
_____
_____
_____
_____
_____
_____
_____
_____
_____
_____
_____
_____
_____

4. _____

_____

_____

_____

_____

_____

_____

_____

_____

_____

_____

_____

_____

_____

_____

_____

5. _____

_____

_____

_____

_____

_____

_____

_____

_____

_____

_____

_____

_____

_____

_____

_____

EXPLORING POSITIVE EMOTIONS (CONTINUED)

Taking into consideration and reflecting on the 5 positive emotions listed previously, as well as the descriptive personal experience of each; contemplate and write down any belief(s) you have in association with the positive emotional response. After identifying the belief, thought pattern, thinking processes, etc., identify how it came into your experience. Is the story you are telling yourself true? Where did it originate?

1. _____
_____
_____
_____
_____
_____
_____
_____
_____
_____

2. _____
_____
_____
_____
_____
_____
_____
_____
_____
_____
_____

3. _____

_____

_____

_____

_____

_____

_____

_____

_____

_____

4. _____

_____

_____

_____

_____

_____

_____

_____

_____

_____

5. _____

_____

_____

_____

_____

_____

_____

_____

_____

_____

After completing the activities and examining our emotions and emotional responses separating the perceived negative from positive experiences, perhaps the most poignant takeaway is recognizing that while we cannot always control our environment and circumstances, we can control our perception, and therefore our emotional response. We find that negative emotions stem from fear and are largely conditional on external metrics, while positive emotions come from a place of love and progress. Clarity comes when we realize that we each have control over our emotions, and therefore how we view the lives we live. If we can control our emotional responses, and our perception of those emotional responses, we have complete control of our lives and our experiences.

Not only do the activities provide us with a better understanding of our emotional responses, and our control in regard to our emotions, but it also serves as the final part of discovery in our self-actualization model. With the last discovery component complete, we have the whole picture. We have a better understanding of who we authentically are, who we want to be and why we want to be that higher-level version of ourselves, independent of outside opinion or influence, and we are free to create the life of health we have always desired, the process with which we have complete control.

17

A NEW APPROACH
ACCOUNTABILITY AND
JOURNALING

Due to the -weight-loss driven focus and paradigm discussed previously, most believe that the caloric deficit is the only real factor to consider to lose weight and decrease body fat. To support that end, many choose to track the calories they consume through food, as well as the estimated calories burned through living, moving, and exercise. As discussed earlier, the numbers rarely equate in weight loss with the mathematical expectation. Further, we find that the reason most folks keep a food and exercise journal is for accountability more than determination of expected results.

Journaling can be an effective process tool in moving us toward who we wish to be, but perhaps journaling and tracking a different metric than what we are used to could lead to a better understanding of the body, facilitate greater gratitude for our bodies, lead to self-appreciation and love, AND potentially move us toward our goals faster!

Having worked previously as a teacher in a Dialectical Behavior Therapeutic (DBT)program, I was introduced to the idea of "Diary Cards" as a system of tracking our emotional responses, and the intensity of said emotions, throughout the day. Additionally, providing any supporting information that may assist in processing to determine what the stimulus was, as well as why we experienced those emotions. The practice has proven effective in assisting people with emotional control and stability. We recognize that calibrating our emotional responses gets easier as we actively try to understand what they are trying to communicate within us.

What if instead of logging our food and exercise, to lose weight (outcome driven); we instead log and rate our emotions to the stimuli of life, activities, experiences, relationships and food?

This kind of regular and consistent self-discovery doesn't come naturally. But like anything in life, the more we practice, the easier it becomes and the better we become. Until we get to the point where self-reflection is unconscious and natural, I suggest the following practice and schedule.

Remove yourself from distraction and record your answers to the following questions. (For the first week, try to do this activity at least every two hours throughout the day. The second week; once every three hours. Weeks 3-4; three times daily, and after a month, once or twice a day will be sufficient as we find the practice becoming more natural and automatic.

What is my current overall mood?
What factors have contributed to my current mood?
Which of those factors can I control?
Am I letting factors out of my control impact my mood?
Is the intensity of my emotional response match the situation?
What is the story I am telling myself about my mood/emotions?
What is the truth? What are the facts?

Consistently asking these questions can be very enlightening. When we live on autopilot geared toward others outcomes, we can never be or do enough; but as we go through this process of self-discovery we find out who we are, who we really want to be, why we want to be that person and allow life to unfold in the most authentic way for each of us. We find balance in Purpose, Intention, Inspiration, and Processes (like the new approach to journalling and others outlined in part 3 of this book) that assist us on our path toward self-actualization.

The bottom ring represents "process." It answers the question "How to I continue to progress?" The center area in which all rings share space represents self actualization and authenticity.

PART 3

RETHINKING OUR APPROACH TO FOOD AND MOVEMENT

18

THE CHANGING NARRATIVES ON DIET AND EXERCISE

Michael Pollan is credited with saying "Our diet has changed more in the last 50 years than the previous 10,000." Even more contrasting is our opinions on what we eat or don't eat for health; as well as what type of exercise we engage in, have changed, and continue to change too often.

With the large focus in the Nutrition and Fitness Industries on selling products and services, it requires new products and novel ideas to perpetuate the sales-focused paradigm discussed earlier. But since that paradigm isn't usually tied to research, science, or health, it allows the narrative, and our beliefs, to also frequently change.

In my four decades of life, I've witnessed fat, protein, and carbohydrates all painted as the "villain" nutrient preventing us from reaching our hoped-for and expected outcomes or results. I've seen, and even trained myself (and others) using, multiple methods and with many rationales: Cardio zone-training, long slow distance, high intensity interval training, yoga, spin, Olympic lifting, power lifting, aerobics, plyometrics and the list could go on and on and on.

We overthink our diet and exercise because we are conditioned to seek faster results with less work. If we collectively had a better understanding of how simple exercise prescription and nutrition can be, and more fully recognized the role of mindset as it relates to diet, exercise, and wellness, we would find ourselves frustrated that we have been conditioned in our beliefs that have dictated our opinions and decisions on diet and exercise. We may even be angry about working-out for decades only to realize that it had little to do with the outcome-'why' we were hoping for! We may be sad that we have led others down a path of misinformation born of our own ignorance. But ultimately, with full understanding we would find a place of inspiration and personal empowerment to create the life that we envision!

We'll examine some commonly held beliefs about diet and exercise, and discuss the truths from myths; and we will outline general fitness and nutrition guidelines to provide simple and realistic systems to encourage us to progress to the most authentically well version of ourselves.

19

A FRESH PERSPECTIVE ON EXERCISE PLANNING

Most exercise prescription models are similar and somewhat outdated. Methods like the FITT principle, periodization schedules, training different energy systems at different times etc. Conventional and traditional programming still works. Research has validated many of these methods; but that doesn't mean there could be a better way. Traditional approaches require time, energy, tracking, planning, functional knowledge of anatomy, and "thick skin" to accept slower than expected results. We validate these messages and methods by calling it "hard work" and saying things like "no pain, no gain." But just because they may work, doesn't mean that there isn't better, faster, and more efficient ways of getting to where we want to be.

Many times, however, indifference is the biggest hindrance in the efficacy of training. We look at environments meant to foster competitive sport prowess like youth recreation and sport leagues through middle and high-school sponsored sports. Unfortunately, most "coaching" is done by volunteers and parents whose fitness and sports training experience is based on their own experience participating in the same sports a generation earlier. We have coaches training their children and students with outdated methods that have, in many circumstances, been shown to decrease performance of said sport! Many times, the methodology, if there is any, stems from the outdated training models.

The FITT principle says basically if one knows the parameters of Frequency (how often), Intensity (how difficult), Time (how long/duration, sets/reps), and Type (the exercise) for the individual components of fitness (Cardio, Strength and Flexibility) than that person *should* be able to design a workout program for him/herself and others. This method still works, and for those who love spending long hours in the gym for consistent, albeit slow, results it's still an option.

Most training programs and protocols are born from the same chaos, confusion, and monetary capitalization discussed earlier.

To satisfy the sales-focused requirement of a novel or new approach, we over-complicate fitness planning.

Yes, personal training works on a personal basis. Yes, periodization works with sport-specific outcomes that lead to success in performing sports or specific skills. But most of the population, by far, just wants to be healthier, move better, and sleep more soundly without pain. Most people don't care about bench pressing a bus, running a sub-five-minute mile, or delivering a flawless gymnastic floor routine. While those other methodologies work and deliver results, the same large majority would get to where they want to be faster, with less effort, by simply switching the way we approach exercise prescription, as well as how we quantify the results. The following solutions are for that "I-just-want-to-feel-better" majority.

Heart Rate Training vs Rate of Perceived Exertion

Heart rate training has become the generally accepted "gold-standard" for cardiovascular development. I remember my high school cross country coach comparing our mileage to money in the bank. "Every mile run is like money in the bank to be withdrawn at State." We were coached that the only way to increase our aerobic conditioning was long-slow-distance or "LSD".

The weight-loss, fitness, and nutrition industries have used similar messaging in terms of general recommendations. We were taught about the "Fat-Burning" heart-rate zone and followed the parameters perfectly toward that outcome; without ever questioning why our results didn't match the expectations or effort. We accepted it without asking more clarifying questions about the role of heart rate and intensity in our total "calories out" as we continued to struggle toward outcome and results. We accepted that "all calories are not equal" as it relates to food, but didn't consider caloric differences in regard to output.

The fat-burning zone does not exist. At least not in the way we have been taught. The first reason I say that it doesn't exist is because it is a metric connected to an outcome, specifically one that we have already discussed earlier about the association of exercise and weight loss. But even if there was a direct and measurable association between calorie burn and weight loss, the "fat burning zone" does not play a role.

The theory states within a specific percentage-of-maximum-heart-rate range, more calories are being burned from fat than carbohydrates. This is true; however, the understanding and application of the knowledge is wildly misrepresented.

For the sake of discussion, let's consider we have two individuals who are biologically identical. We'll call them Tim and Tom. They see eye-to-eye when it comes to most things, however Tim believes in the fat burning zone and Tom does not.

Tim and Tom both enjoy running and have 20 minutes for their runs. Tim is careful to stay in his "fat-burning zone" and runs at 4 miles per hour and covers approximately 1.3 miles. Tom runs at 6 miles per hour, and subsequently covers 2 miles. 65% of Tim's calories come from fat, while 35% come from carbohydrates. Only 50% of Tom's calories come from fat, and 50% come from carbohydrates. If we stopped the comparison here, it would seem clear that Tim is more effective by staying in his zone. At the end of their 20-minute runs, Tim burned 200 total calories, with 130 coming from fat, while Tom burned a total of 280 calories, with 140 coming from fat. Tom, running at a level higher that the fat-burning zone burned not only more total calories, but also more calories from fat!

Heart rate has proven to be a poor metric for exercise prescription and quantification based on other factors as well. Those with prescribed medication for high blood pressure aren't able to use heart rate because the medication controls the heart rate. Similarly, caffeine is a regularly consumed stimulant, and will increase the heart rate, making heart rate training less accurate.

Even if heart-rate training did work the way we have been taught, newer emerging science is showing that there may be a better way. Research is showing that short-duration, high-intensity interval training (anaerobic) elicits greater cardiorespiratory adaptations in the body, than traditional "cardio." Sometimes it's not about working harder and longer, but instead smarter.

Instead of using heart rate, Rate of Perceived Exertion (RPE scale) is an easier and more accurate means of assessment. The RPE scale is a scale from 1-10 on how hard we feel we are working. Perhaps the strongest argument for using the RPE method is that since no two workouts are the same, it is impossible to measure them against a standard that is continuously moving as well. Additionally, regardless of the technologies used by our watches and heart rate monitors, none of them can reflect how we feel, or how motivated we are, or how fatigued we are. RPE provides a universal language to quantify what we are doing, and more importantly how we feel while we are doing it.

When we aren't focused on all of the quantitative metrics and prescriptive factors in our exercise and movement, it allows us to be more present, and enjoy the experience in the moment rather than allowing the outcome to determine our experience.

Strength Intervals vs Sets and Reps

After looking at how simple changes in cardio prescription and quantification can be; it brings up similar questions about traditional methods of strength training prescription and quantification. Strength training messages have changed over years and decades in the same way as nutrition and cardio. There are weight training protocols for "bulking", or "cutting". Different programs for developing Speed and Power vs Strength and Endurance. Much of strength training is tied to aesthetic outcomes, while some is based on rehabilitation of movement etc. Because the intention behind our strength program is often misguided, we utilize recommendations that may not be the best for us; and in most cases aren't tied to what it is that we really are hoping to achieve. What about most folks who just want to move their bodies to maintain general health? Is there an easier way; one that doesn't require an extensive knowledge of functional anatomy and physiology, with predetermined sets and reps at a specific weight of exercises that targets specific muscles? Can Movement prescription for Strength be just as easy as the RPE scale for Cardio? It can; but it does require looking at exercise through a completely different lens than before.

This idea is not new or novel; but its application to movement and "exercise" progression is. Although it's first applications date back to Galileo and the Renaissance, the concept was not fully understood until the early 1800s when French mathematician Gaspard-Gustave Coriolis defined *Work* as "weight lifted through a height" although it was not applied the same way we would read that definition today; as he was looking at steam engine's ability to remove water from flooded mines, and not pressing a bar from ones chest. Although not originally intended to be used in this way, I love this original definition applied to our movement and our capacity to do work, aka move our bodies, and quantify the amount of work we do.

Let's start by talking about the word Work. We are using the word in terms of its mathematical connotation as the measurable output of a movement or exercise; and not something that "we have to do" toward an outcome. I also realize that there are other considerations regarding the physics approach that we won't discuss; not because it's not relevant, but rather, the intention is to provide an easy and quick method to measure our individual progress.

Upon considering the mathematical and scientific relevance introduced by Galileo and Coriolis, we can examine a few ways that we can apply this to our movement patterns and our exercise protocols. This approach may even be more effective at increasing our total work, with less negative impact on the body, and change our approach to exercise and the ego associated with outcome. We will further discuss this new means of measuring our movement, but first, let's consider some exercise programming suggestions that support this new way of thinking about exercise and movement.

Variability

We have all heard that practice makes perfect. We have experienced the more we repeat something, the more natural and automatic it becomes; but a basic misunderstanding of exercise and metabolism has led to plateaus in our wellness journeys, and therefore frustration with why we are not where we feel like we should be, even when doing everything "right". The misunderstanding spoken of is thinking our bodies were created and have evolved to "burn" energy instead of "conserving" energy.

This misunderstanding is largely due to the outcome-focused mentality that drives our decisions and actions. When we hit fitness plateaus on our wellness journeys, how do we perceive them? Are we happy about the plateau? Usually we view a plateau as negative, but that is exactly what our bodies are conditioned to do; regardless of whether it's what we want or not! So, if we intend to subvert the natural physiological response to conserve energy, attempt to prevent the body from efficiently storing fat for future energy, and instead utilize our already stored fat for energy, we must add variety to everything we do and the way we do it. We have to vary our exercises, as well as the frequency and intensity.

This flies in the face of commonly utilized fitness programming models. We hear things like: "Monday and Wednesday is Arms and Abs, Tuesday and Thursday is Legs and Back" or "20 minutes of cardio followed by 2 sets of 12 reps" of selected exercise(s). We find most traditional programs are very repetitive; and as a result, don't lead to the results we feel we earned, or we get bored and start looking for something else.

As we look around today, it's not a coincidence that the most popular programs (that people are enjoying and getting results) are based on the "daily" workout model, in which the only time a complete workout is repeated is if it is a benchmark workout to serve as future reference of improvement. It's been called "Muscle confusion" by some programs, or "WOD" meaning Workout of the Day, but regardless of the marketing twists, we are talking about the same thing; the principle of Variability and suffice to say switch up your routine as often as possible! Looking at the previously mentioned definition of insanity, we find that the alternative to this new approach is merely more of the same, disappointment or frustration from unrealized and unmet external outcomes and expectations.

Choose multi-joint functional movements to increase efficacy and decrease time.

I realize the statement appears to be like thousands of other claims. I know it sounds fanciful that anything could be more effective and save time and energy. But let me explain my rationale; how I came to this conclusion. The statement talks of just two-qualifiers; "multi-joint" and "functional", and it's important we understand these qualifiers.

Most traditional training models are based around exercises meant to target individual body parts or muscles. We have "arm day" or "leg day" and pick exercises that correspond with those muscles; and subsequently go through the motions of designated sets and reps. There is nothing inherently wrong with this approach, and it has helped many get to their goals, but there is a better way, and it begins with choosing different movements. The more joints involved in a movement, the higher is output and therefore efficacy. Additionally, multi-joint functional movements are more closely aligned with how we move throughout the day. When choosing exercises and movements, I only include those that either stabilize or articulate three or more joints of the seven I consider (Ankles, Knees, Hips, Spine, Shoulders Elbows, Wrists)

Functional movements can be defined as those movements which enhance our quality of life and strengthen the body specific to the way we move. The truth is many common exercises are not functional; and in many cases are causing movement imbalance, dysfunction, and injuries.

After considering variability in programming and choosing movements that use multiple joints and are functional, we can discuss how this different way to quantify our exercise leads to better and faster results.

When we use the physics definition of work to dictate our decisions about our exercises, the first thing we recognize is how simple and easy the *planning* becomes as we realize there is none. We don't have to remember how much weight we can lift for specific exercises. We don't have to know how many sets and reps to do of certain exercises. We don't have to have an in-depth knowledge of anatomy; the muscles and the exercises meant to stimulate and strengthen specific muscles. Instead, we just have to recognize functional movement patterns, and plug them into any interval training format and that becomes the "workout." It requires very little time, effort, and knowledge to put the workout together, but will generate greater progress.

To illustrate this point let's compare and contrast two common exercises: the bicep curl, and the Thruster.

The Bicep curl articulates only one joint. It is targeted to stimulate the muscle(s) that flex the elbow, that also have a more limited capacity. So, the output when the force and distance is calculated, is very little. Plugged into a normal "workout" the bicep curl will usually be performed for 2-3 sets of 8-12 reps: taking a lot of time, and accomplishing limited and little actual work.

The thruster is the name of a compound movement that combines a front squat followed by an overhead press. The thruster is a multi-joint (that incorporates all seven joints previously mentioned) and functional movement. In addition to the added joints involved in the movement, the limbs and move through a wider range of motion, and lift more weight utilizing more of the body, so the "work" output is exponentially greater. We find that one repetition of the thruster elicits up to 300x more "work" than one repetition of a bicep curl. Furthermore, when we plug thrusters into a Tabata interval format, we find that the total work in that four minutes is greater than we find in 60-90 minutes of conventional workouts based on sets and reps.

Not only do multi-joint functional movements lead to greater progress; they also have much less potentially negative impact on the body. Functional movements enhance the coordination and efficiency of the body, however dysfunctional movements introduce forces onto the body's joints, muscles and connective tissue at greater levels and in ways the body has not evolved to efficiently move, ultimately increasing the risk of muscle imbalance and injury. Functional movements are safer, and when we plug them into an interval system, it forces us to use less weight than we would if doing a "sets and reps" strength workout; and with less weight and resistance, also puts less impact on the body.

This may lead one to ask: "wouldn't that lead to less results?" That seemingly obvious question is the result of the outcome-focused paradigm discussed earlier in the book but can be answered easily by applying this new method of measuring our exercise output.

Let's use a different exercise to answer that question by looking at the Bench Press. Consider that a person's one-rep-max bench Press is 225#. One-Rep-Max is a marker that means it takes max effort to lower the bar and press it back just one time. That single rep, while it can provide valuable information, does have a much higher risk level due to the body, muscles, tendons, and joints not being conditioned to that intensity, coupled with a higher risk of cardiac event because breath is usually held during the rep.

Suppose our subject removed the four 45-pound plates from the barbell, and instead only bench pressed the empty (45-pound) barbell. Since the range of motion (distance) is the same whether pressing 45 pounds or 225 pounds, the weight (force) is the only factor to consider here. Based on the logic of the physics definition of work, our subject produces the same amount of work in bench pressing the 225# bar once, or the 45# bar 5 times. But they can do many more sets of 5 with an empty bar, than sets of 1 with the maximally loaded bar; and can do so with much less risk.

Another acknowledgment we discover in letting go of the outcome-focused approach exercise, and looking at movement through the lens of intention; we find that the body does know when we are exercising, or resting, or working etc. Our bodies continually respond to the external and environmental stimuli placed on us. The body doesn't differentiate whether we are walking on a stair-stepper at the gym, or whether we are walking up a set of stairs at work. Whether we are running on a treadmill for fitness training, or whether we are running away from danger. Taken a step further, whether we have a

60-minute block for exercise, 10 6-minute blocks, 6 ten-minute blocks or 60 1 minute blocks, it all "counts" equally. And in most cases, participating in movement in small bouts throughout the day, as opposed to longer-gym sessions, usually results in more work, and faster progress in the direction of wellness.

Components of Fitness

Any remaining confusion around this approach to fitness programming is likely due to our understanding, and misunderstanding, of energy systems, and the components of fitness. Most training protocols are based around energy systems (Fat Metabolism/Oxidation, Anaerobic glycolysis, aerobic glycolysis, Phospho-Creatine etc.) or fitness components (Cardio, Strength, Flexibility, and Body Composition). As a result, we have predetermined exercises that *should* lead to generally accepted and expected outcomes, which sometimes are, but mostly aren't, associated with those desired outcomes.

We already discussed the benefits of using RPE over Heart rate, anaerobic high-intensity over cardio long slow distance, and multi-joint functional movements as intervals, instead of isolated, sometimes dysfunctional, movements. It's important however to understand that our bodies have the capacity to train and condition more than one energy system at a time or more than one component at a time. We don't have to separate our cardio from strength, or flexibility from cardio, and so on.

Not only do our bodies can increase fitness concurrently across all components and systems, but it's also actually more functional and realistic, and it forces us to not prioritize one component over another. Cardio-respiratory endurance is usually considered the most important component of fitness, followed by muscular strength and endurance, while flexibility is often not even considered. My personal belief and recommendation are to reverse that order.

I believe in a foundation of flexibility, as the most important component, for several reasons. Most importantly, if one has "good" flexibility and mobility, (meaning they can move the joints of their body freely through their range of motion, without pain or injury) that person will get more out of their cardio and strength, while if there are limitations to flexibility, those imbalances or weaknesses will contribute to limitations in movement and impact quality of life. Secondly, if we remove the outcome-focus of our diet and exercise habits, and look at our real intention, we find that we really just want to be able to use our bodies in ways that we are currently limited; and usually those factors have more to do with flexibility than they do our ability to run a 5-minute mile, or bench press 400 pounds. Lasty we now understand that there is very little association between exercise-burned calories and weight-loss, so regardless of how we prioritize the components of fitness in our planning, it's a very small part of the puzzle as it relates to body composition changes.

If we start with the foundation of flexibility, change the way we approach cardio metrics using the RPE instead of heart rate, using varied multi-joint functional movements in intervals rather than sets and reps of the same exercises, we find how easy it is to live a life directed by the processes of purpose, instead of falling victim to the culture of outcome.

20

A FRESH PERSPECTIVE ON NUTRITION PLANNING

I am not a nutritionist, and I am not a dietician, so I am limited in my dietary recommendations, and recognize that my opinions in regard to food are just that; which is probably best as my views and opinions on diet are dynamic and changing. I have fallen victim to societal messaging discussed earlier, and have allowed the way I've eaten, and food in general, to be a source of rigidity and dogmatism through most of my life. I believed the way I was eating was the best for me, others, the environment and the world. And I had strong beliefs about those who didn't agree with my point of view, or at least felt like others were ignorant for not even trying to see it my way.

For me, that all changed when I was challenged and asked "why" by my friend, life-long learner, and nutritionist, Melissa. It was the first time that I considered my motivation or intention about my diet. I was convinced that my way was the "healthiest" and therefore best, and sought information and research that validated my belief, so why even consider "why" I was eating the way I was? That holier-than-thou mentality crumbled when I was simply asked to consider why I was eating a certain way. Melissa's posed question was about research that I hadn't, or wasn't willing to look at, regarding the "health" argument of my approach. Being asked that simple "why" served a much greater purpose as the catalyst of asking "why" in other aspects of my life, ultimately leading to the overarching message of this work. I share this not only because it was such a pivotal point in my life, but also to clarify that my now more-dynamic approach to food and recommendations are not mine. I want to ensure that credit is given where credit is due, which for this segment, largely belongs to Melissa, her quest to for self-improvement, and desire to add value to the lives of those she meets.

Like other themes of this work, I don't believe that there is any diet (system of eating) that is optimal for every individual person. Furthermore, nutrition science and research is revealing that the optimal diet for each person may be as unique as we each all individually are. This is great news for those of us attempting to live, move, and eat more authentically and intentionally. When we can remove the outcome(s) associated with our food and eating habits, we're able to begin examining *why* we are eating the way we are. Through examining our intention, we can replace scarcity mindset with abundance, rules with freedom, guidelines with choice, and ultimately begin to recognize the role food plays in our emotions and hormonal regulation, biological, physiological, and metabolic processes; and not limited to the (mostly) arbitrary number of calories.

The following recommendation may seem simple, especially based on the food-related messaging that regularly bombards us in nearly every part of our lives. But once we are able to really recognize that most of our food beliefs and habits are cultural and societal phenomena, and let go of outcomes and expectations associated with our food, we find that perhaps a simple approach is the most authentic path to contentment in our relationships with food.

Food and Emotions

The relationship between food and emotions is vast and dynamic, and we are continually learning more about how interwoven they are. The more we understand this relationship, the more we recognize how much we have gotten wrong about food; It's the adage attributed to Einstein "the more I learn, the more I realize I don't know." If we want to create the best system of nutrition for ourselves, we must begin by acknowledging our emotions as they relate to our food, our cravings, eating, and satiety. And since the "perfect diet" doesn't exist, we must each look at our relationship with food, and honestly ask and answer the hard questions ourselves.

It is well documented that our emotions do influence dietary behaviors. Both negative and positive emotions can lead to cravings, as well as eating and food-related behaviors like restriction or binging. The frequency and intensity in which we feel specific emotions (like joy and anger) is directly associated with the level of the craving, restriction, eating or other food-related behavior. The volatility and range of the associations between food and emotions are the central reason we must begin by recognizing and acknowledging the relationship for ourselves, individually.

We are not taught about Emotional Intelligence, at least to the level that we as society need. As a result we either don't use emotional feedback in our day to day actions, behaviors, and decisions, or we wait until those emotional signals are extreme at either end. This disconnect is observable in our eating behaviors and lives. For example, emotional hunger is very different from physical hunger, as well as the associated triggers, cravings, and satiety; all discussed in the next section.

Hunger Scale and Emotional Calibration to the Hunger Scale

Before introducing how the "hunger scale" works, it's important to acknowledge the differences between emotional and physical hunger.

Physical hunger gradually increases without any urgency or triggering event until food is available, while emotional hunger feels urgent in nature, and is usually associated with a triggering event like poor sleep, stress or work that leads to the urgency. Emotional hunger is associated with craving certain (usually unhealthful) foods, while physical hunger is tied to physical conditions like stomach "rumbling", and not associated with commonly craved foods.

Not only can we differentiate between emotional and physical hunger, we can also contrast our emotional responses to physical vs emotional hunger. Physical hunger is typically not associated with an emotional response, but rather just an observance of the body and its processes. Emotional hunger stems from non-digestive or metabolic processes, so the responses are emotional in nature; and are most commonly emotions like shame, guilt, unworthiness etc. We realize it really isn't about the food or the craving as much as what the food and craving represents, or what it was born from.

Understanding the role of emotions in our diet becomes easier when looking at it from an evolutionary biology standpoint. Doug Lisle in his book "The Dietary Pleasure Trap" explains that humans are hard-wired to seek pleasure and avoid pain. The dopaminergic response associated with sugar and fat is as influential as it appears to be with narcotics and alcohol. As a result, the body and brain start to identify the little-work-high-reward association, and we (temporarily) feel good! "We make the wrong decision and the body thinks it's the right one… Then later on we reverse direction and change our diets and make the body feels like it's the wrong decision"

If we intend to eat with intention, we must start by observing our emotions regarding everything associated with food. If we don't begin with an understanding of our individual emotional responses to food, we are once again seeking solutions outside of ourselves toward an outcome, and as a result remain chasing a moving target.

The hunger scale is a tool that helps differentiate between emotional and physical hunger, and rate that hunger on a numeric scale from one to ten with 1 being nearly empty, 10 stuffed full, and 5 right where you would expect, neither hungry nor full. The hunger scale is for identifying the level of physical hunger and has been used for traditional body-composition approaches, although for the purposes of this book, we intend to dig a little deeper. In identifying the level of physical hunger, it allows us to consider our emotional associations with our eating. Knowing our hunger triggers allow us to ask addition questions instead of just rating our hunger. A couple of examples of questions that identify physical hunger and acknowledge emotions are:

"Am I feeding my body, or filling my belly?"

"To what degree am I attempting to not feel something?"

"Is this _____ what my body wants and needs, or I am using it to escape of cover up?"

Nutrient Density

Perhaps the most disingenuous disservice from the food industry's messaging is the oversimplified and unfounded concept of calories' role in energy balance. A diet based on the number of calories is not one that will lead to continued and/or lasting results. It does not serve as an effective method because it is not the number of calories that determines or contributes to health or sickness, but rather what those calories are composed of, or their nutrient density. Nutrient density is defined as the ratio of beneficial micro and macro nutrients to the item's total energy/calories.

Today's food sources have lower nutrient density than in the past resulting in a population state of nutrient deficiency and caloric surplus. Even whole foods are less nutrient rich due to environmental concerns like deforestation, climate change, topsoil loss, genetically modified organisms, and systems of farming etc., so even historically "healthy" food is less so. It's a vicious pattern, and nearly impossible to combat with the current societal messaging on calories.

Because of the frustration we deal with regarding messaging, people often throw their hands up and say: "just tell me what to eat and what not eat" seeking externally which foods are "healthy" vs "unhealthy". The problem with this approach is not only that it is externally focused on moving targets, but more so that food, like other concepts in this book, is not black and white. Everything we consume is on scale.

Let's consider what we eat on the nutrient density continuum. This allows us each to recognize our attitudes and intention behind eating the way we do, understand the implications associated with eating, and making a conscious decision to consume the item or not consume it based on how it may affect each of us. It also allows our perception and mindset to dictate what we feel is best for us individually.

As a general rule of thumb when considering our food, the more natural state the item, the more nutrient dense, and the more processed, the less nutrient dense it is. The greater the number of ingredients, the less nutrient dense, and the fewer the ingredients, the better the choice etc.

I know it's not a meal plan with specific rules and requirements, but diet was not intended to be a limiting factor to our lives, but a catalyst for life experience, and if saying "eat food that makes you happy" is a little too "hippy dippy free spirited" in regard to meal planning, we can dig a little deeper and get a little more specific with some other tips, tricks, and suggestions based on the latest science and research.

Matching Macronutrients with Vegetables

Like exercise, there is no diet that is going to be perfect for everyone because everyone is unique but also each person's intention is different. Most of the messaging on diet is specific to losing weight, but if we remove the outcome and look at diet as feeding our bodies to move and operate most efficiently, it allows us to meal plan just as individually as we all are.

Societal messaging and conditioning have taught us that diet planning isn't any easier than sticking to a diet, even though it can and should be. I had no idea just how easy until I heard my friend and nutrition guru explain the concept by simply saying: "Match your servings of any macro nutrient, with a serving of vegetables." Essentially half of the food we consume (by volume, not calories) should be vegetables, or when we look at our plate, half is filled with our protein(s), carbohydrate(s), and fat(s), and the other half is filled with (non-starchy) vegetables! For each serving of carbohydrate, protein, or fat we consume, we should also have a serving of vegetables. It's a simple approach that acknowledges all of the considerations such as satiety, nutrient density, individual preference and taste, etc. and when we are eating that volume of whole plant-based foods, the total number of calories is much lower than most be expect based on how they feel.

Shopping for Food - The twenty-item shopping list

One frustration in diet and meal planning is shopping. Most diet programs have stringent rules that dictate what to buy and not buy, how much to buy, etc. A traditional approach is to create a meal plan, and then purchase all the individual ingredients to prepare those meals. This approach may work for some, but it does require more time and energy, is usually more expensive, and typically leads to more wasted food. Instead of this cumbersome process, an opposite approach like the twenty-item shopping list may be just the solution.

List your five-favorite carbohydrates, fats, proteins and non-starchy vegetables. Those twenty items are your shopping list and can provide limitless possibilities for meal creation! Let me explain.

Let's say my five carbohydrates are: tortillas, pasta, pita, whole grain bread and rice; they go on the list. And then we can add 5 protein sources: tuna, chicken, eggs, lentils, and beef; they go on the list. Following the same process for fats: nuts, avocado, cheese, butter, and oil. Lastly, I can pick 5 non-starchy vegetables: green leafy veg of some kind, carrots, cauliflower, baby peppers, and some kind of squash. I haven't added spices, or flavor enhancing foods like garlic, onion, lemon etc., which of course are also welcome and great to use with this type of food preparation.

With only those twenty items, I have limitless possibilities to create many different meal options. I could make chicken fajitas, tuna melt, cheesy cauliflower pasta, avocado toast, etc. and the list goes on and on. It forces us to get creative with what we eat and how we prepare it. In that creativity we end up getting nutrients from an array of sources. If this method is coupled with the hunger-scale and vegetable matching it provides a framework for progress and nutrient efficiency without calorie counting, and with limited planning. In short, a real-life solution that can be maintained and eventually adopted into habit.

Water

Drinking water is something we all know we should be doing more of, and I believe it is the key to much of what is holding back our progress. Water is tied to health, nutrient absorption, body system efficiency, immunity, food satiety, etc. As a general recommendation, drink water based on the ratio of fluid ounces to pounds of body weight (.5:1 ≤ 1:1). Simply put, a 200-pound person should aim to get between 100-200 fluid ounces of water each day!

Supplementation

As discussed earlier in the book, health has been marginalized and capitalized with a focus on generating revenue as the greatest priority. A huge portion of this is the largely unregulated supplement industry. However, this doesn't mean that there aren't benefits to the supplementation of micronutrients (vitamins and minerals) and macronutrients. But with all the mixed messaging, how can we really know what to supplement, and the appropriate method(s) and dosing? And are all "like" supplements created equal?

We need to approach supplementation in the same vein as has been discussed with diet and exercise; there is no magic pill or singular solution. If claims sound to-good-to-be-true, they probably are. But just as applicable as with food and movement, every supplement will affect and impact every individual differently, which means our approach and utilization of supplements should also be unique and individual.

A former colleague of mine, pharmacist, and leader in his field, Dr. Koby Taylor, suggests a similar individualized approach, based on individual *deficiency*, as well as specific medical, clinical, and/or psychological diagnoses. Instead of a conventional symptomatic 'take-this-for-that" method. Our physical bodies are designed to work efficiently without disease. When medical conditions arise, they do so because of some kind of imbalance, somewhere. Rather than the traditional band-aid approach, we would benefit greatly by looking at what nutrient deficiencies, and behaviors, are associated with our condition and experience.

Once we approach supplementation based on our own individual deficiencies and/or imbalances, our priority then becomes sourcing and quality. In any industry we understand that not all products are equal, but this is especially true with supplements due to the dysregulated "wild west" nature of the industry. It is paramount that each person researches any supplement, medication or compound put in the body. This "research" should include the considerations: "*What* are the intended outcome(s) for this and *Why* should I take this?" "What is the appropriate dosing for me and my goals, and how/what are the metrics to track actual benefits?" "Are the effects/

benefits reachable through food alone?" and if not "do the effects/benefits merit the costs associated?"

Even with this guidance, it is important to remember that supplementation should be just that; to supplement something missing or out of balance for the limited time of the imbalance or deficiency, and our supplement programs should be regularly re-evaluated and modified accordingly.

Afterword

I've spent a lot of energy and intention merging my experience and perspective in writing this book, and so I believed that upon completing it I would feel a sense of closure or accomplishment. But that's not at all what happened, at least not yet. Instead of an end, I've found ideas of other beginnings. Instead of closure and accomplishment, I've found expansion and excitement. I had hoped that in completing the book, I would have a concise and powerful ending, but instead have more questions myself then I ever imagined the reader considering.

I suppose it shouldn't come as a surprise, as continued personal introspection and intention are main themes. Should writing down my ideas and thoughts as a book excuse myself of living conducive to the message? In fact, perhaps the biggest takeaway is that I wrote this for me. While it was written from "our" perspective and posed rhetorical questions to "us"; really it was just the Universe's, or God's way of getting me to look at my shadows and blind spots. That's what I continue to plan on doing with these pages; revisiting the principles and processes as I progress toward self-actualization and joyful-intentional- authenticity, and hope that it serves others in the same spirit it has me.

Printed in the United States
by Baker & Taylor Publisher Services